A BODY
in Redwork

More from the
Missouri Star Mystery Series

Chain Piecing a Mystery
A Body in Redwork

Serial novellas published in
Missouri Star Quilt Co.- BLOCK magazine

Mystery in the Old Quilt
Bound in Secrets and Lies

Hillary Doan Sperry

A BODY
in Redwork

1

Jenny waffled between pure joy and worry all day long. Now she stood at the window watching a light snow fall on the sidewalk. Her friends would be arriving any minute and she couldn't help second guessing herself.

It had been weeks since she'd accidentally double booked herself, planning a quilting retreat for friends the same week as the first official designers convention at her family's company, the Missouri Star Quilt Co. She would play a heavy role in both and hadn't gone a day without wondering if still hosting the retreat was the right thing to do.

"Do you think I should have postponed?" The retreat girls hadn't even arrived yet and already she'd seen three popular designers walking past the rental she had booked. "This is going to be a good thing, right?"

Cherry Carmine, Jenny's assistant, continued arranging stacks of fabric and sewing tools on the eight sewing tables they'd set up in the large dining room. "Of course. Everyone's more excited to meet the *sew*-lebrities than we are to be sewing anyway." Cherry looked up, eyes wide and glanced at Jenny. "But you didn't hear that from me."

Jenny laughed, letting some of her worry go. "But it won't be good if I'm hardly around, either."

She didn't really have a say in when the designers convention was happening but keeping the retreat going worried Jenny. She didn't want her friends to be upset if she had to be gone every night.

Cherry joined her at the window. Her vibrant red blouse caught Jenny's eye and she turned to her friend. The patterned blouse was as bright red as her name, with white quilter's stars all over it. The color picked up the red tones in her blonde hair and was perfect for the Redwork Retreat that was starting as soon as the rest of her friends showed up.

Cherry bumped Jenny's shoulder lightly, her soft Southern accent making everything feel a little cozier. "I know you're worried about being busy, but everyone will understand. You only have one event most days anyway. You'll get to spend all day with us sewing before you have to go put on a show for the rest of the town." Cherry's reassurance confirmed what she'd been telling herself.

It was going to be fine.

Jenny took a deep breath. Cherry's homemade cinnamon cider was bubbling on the stove and had filled the room with its sharp spicy fragrance. It filled her up, and as Jenny let her breath out she relaxed. Again. "The shows are pretty fun."

"And everyone is going to be there, right? Did

Andi take care of tickets?" Cherry's smile pinched and she tried not to notice as Cherry picked up the last stack of precut fabrics from the box and waved it at her. "There's only a handful of us and we're still going to need more fabric bundles. How does that happen?"

Her cheery tone belied the underlying frustration Cherry held for the situation. Only a couple months earlier, Cherry had saved a friend's life at the expense of a severely broken bone. She'd only recently made it out of her cast and still couldn't lift much more than the small pack of fabric she was currently carrying. Because of Cherry's injury Jenny had enlisted the help of another assistant, but Cherry wasn't thrilled with sharing her responsibilities.

"Andi did get the tickets, right?" Cherry looked over her shoulder as she placed the last of the fabric in front of a sewing machine.

"I think so." Jenny turned a spool of red thread in her hand and looked around the dining room. "I hope we're ready."

The finished tables were set with bundles of red and white tone on tone prints and the patterns that they would start tomorrow, their first official retreat day. They'd be working on a redwork table runner, something small to get people going. She'd even included a little accessory bundle for each guest - she didn't have the bundles yet, but Andi had promised to send them over. She thought about the list of projects they had provided and started to smile again. It was only Monday, and they had a whole week of laughter and fun ahead of them.

The front door creaked loudly behind them, and both women turned. After a bit of shuffling in the entry, Jenny glanced at Cherry and moved forward to see who had arrived. "Maura? Tilly?" Jenny called off the names of some of her expected guests. "Do you need any—Oh!"

Just as the new arrival had started to respond they both turned the corner and walked into each other. The woman who rounded the corner lost her grip on the box she was carrying and tumbled to the ground as she called out, startled.

"Oh my goodness!" Her blonde hair fell around her shoulders as she bent to save the box. Red and white fabric and ruler templates scattered on the ground.

"Let me help." Cherry and Jenny both hurried forward and began picking up supplies.

When the woman's head lifted Jenny leaned back, surprised. "Sally? What are you doing here?"

A wide smile spread across Sally's face. "I wasn't expecting to see you here, either. I can take care of this. You don't need to be down here."

Sally tried to shoo her away from the box but Jenny resisted, holding up a pack of fabric that matched the ones they'd just run out of.

"I think you can read minds. How did you know we needed these?"

"I was just helping out." Sally was closing the box top on the sewing tools and pointed around the

4

house. "Hugo was helping Andi, and he got busy or something. I'm just the messenger," she said, holding up her hands.

Jenny's brow furrowed. "Oh, strange. I thought I saw him walking down the street earlier."

Sally shrugged and held up the box. "Where would you like them?"

"You can set those anywhere over there," Cherry said, pointing toward the kitchen and scooping up the last piece of fabric. Sally crossed the dining room while Jenny and Cherry followed slowly.

Cherry leaned over and whispered, "Do we know her?"

Jenny almost laughed. For as much as Cherry and she had been through, she sometimes forgot that they'd been working together less than a year. Despite some dangerous situations, Cherry's arm was evidence that they had become fast friends. But it wasn't the crazy things that made her feel like family. It was the friendship that had grown between them. Sewing together, laughing, going on shopping trips, trying new things. Cherry had been by her side since she'd been hired, and it hadn't taken long for Jenny to realize it wasn't just a job to Cherry. She genuinely loved what she did, and Jenny was grateful to have found her.

"Cherry Carmine," Jenny gestured to Sally as she met them back in the dining room. "This is Sally Harper. She's the owner of Harper Wovens, one of their first designers, and a good friend."

"Co-owner," Sally clarified, her pale hair

swinging around her shoulders. "I have a partner that likes to work behind the scenes."

Cherry didn't say anything for a moment. Jenny leaned over prodding her and Cherry blinked, then nodded her head toward Jenny as if nothing had happened. "Me too. Jenny is all behind the scenes. She never wants to get out."

The heavy sarcasm brought on a round of laughter. Sally and Jenny typically found each other at events and in other towns, since Jenny traveled so often for quilting events and shows.

"Oh, I can see that. This woman barely sees the light of day, doesn't she?" Sally chuckled and held out her hand. "Ms. Carmine, I believe it's very nice to meet you."

"I like her." Cherry said, shaking Sally's hand firmly. "Thank you so much for bringing the supplies. I'm sure you're busy getting ready for the designers convention."

"It is busy. In fact, Owen, my co-owner of Harper Wovens, he's going to be missing me. I should probably get back and help him get the booth set up. It's a good thing he likes me." Sally straightened her shirt hem and gave Jenny a hug. "Good luck with the retreat, and say hi to Mickey for me. She's not picking up calls again. I'm anxious to see her."

It was said with good humor and Jenny waved to Sally as the door creaked shut behind her. Mickey was one of Jenny's friends that had recently joined Sally's company as a fabric designer. It was fun to see one of her friends succeeding like that.

Cherry stood watching the door. "She owns Harper and Wovens?"

Jenny nodded and went into the kitchen to see what else was in the box. Cherry wasn't paying attention as she followed and bumped into the table.

"You alright?" Jenny tried to help Cherry focus. "Cause I need you to help me put these things out. The first group of girls are going to get here any minute."

Cherry shook her head lightly and seemed to come back to herself. "That was Sally Harper. The owner of Harper Wovens. Wow. I really love this job. However, could you warn me next time we're hosting top fabric designers?" She fluffed her hair slightly and let her southern accent take on more of a twang as she teased Jenny. "I might have curled my hair."

Jenny stacked fabric and cutting mats to carry out to the sewing tables and tried not to smile too big. "I'm afraid there will be a lot of that this week."

Jenny had known Sally since her first years in the fabric industry. With everything Harper Wovens handled, Jenny sometimes forgot how popular she was as a designer.

At one point Jenny had thought she would design fabric too - she'd even attempted some artwork a few times, but it wasn't in the cards for her. She shook off the longing as Cherry passed her, setting up another table with patterns and sewing swag.

"It looks amazing." Cherry put her hands on her hips and looked at Jenny. "You're getting really good at this."

By the time the first guests arrived Cherry and Jenny had begun experimenting with how many ways you could wear the various sewing supplies that had been provided for the retreat guests. Jenny was in a full belly laugh at Cherry's attempt to turn a template into a hat, tied down with a measuring tape and binding clips when the first knock came. Cherry shushed her as she put away the supplies and Jenny hurried to the front door.

The snow hadn't gone away and a thin layer covered the grass and sidewalks.

Tilly stood on the porch, the young woman's brown hair in loose waves down her back and her bags piled around her. Maura was next to Tilly, a single duffle hitched over her shoulder and a small clear bin of fabric at her hip. Maura was in her mid-forties, her hair a wash of blond, brown, and gray that looked like the color of wheat fields in the rain.

"You cut your hair!" Jenny said to Maura, opening her arms to hug her.

Maura swished her chin length locks as she moved inside. "Do you like it? I haven't had it short in years. I think I love it."

Tilly pulled her bags into the entryway. Her youth and excitement radiated through the exhaustion in her eyes.

"I can't believe you made it!" Jenny pulled Tilly into a hug of her own. "I didn't know if you'd be able to get away from all those babies." Tilly relaxed into the embrace, and a small moan escaped her. "I can't tell you how good it is to be here."

Then, as if exhaustion was a feeling she could turn off with a switch, she jumped back and clapped her hands. "You would not believe who we saw on the way in."

When Jenny didn't respond, Tilly launched into the room, talking as she went.

"Hugo Hensen was standing on Main Street. Right on the corner down from here."

"Wow." Jenny followed her.

"Hey, I know Hugo," Cherry said from the sewing room.

Tilly's brows rose. "Really? What's he like?"

Cherry's mouth dropped open. "Oh, no. I didn't mean, I meant, well, I just really like his work—" Cherry stepped forward and held out her hand. "Hi, I'm Cherry. I've never met Hugo Hensen or any other famous fabric designers. Well, maybe one." She glanced at Jenny and Tilly was speechless for half a second before bursting out laughing.

She took Cherry's hand briefly. "I'm Tilly." She gave Cherry and Jenny a conflicted look. "Right now Hugo Hensen is only two blocks away, and I'm dragging torn luggage into a house full of women."

Maura snorted in the background. "Come on, Tilly. I'm as good-looking as he is!"

Jenny savored the light-hearted exchange as Tilly pulled her things toward the stairs. She hadn't thought about how much her friends would enjoy getting to see their favorite designers and sew-lebrities in person. She was suddenly grateful that she hadn't moved the retreat after all.

A car door slammed, and Jenny looked outside. Mickey's slim figure and ginger red hair were climbing out of a dark sports car.

Stepping out onto the porch Jenny called to the younger woman. "Why are you driving that? It's winter."

Mickey turned, her jeans and sweater looking far more casual than her car indicated. "I got an advance, and I was excited." She jogged to meet Jenny as she came down the porch steps.

"An advance?" She hadn't heard of that in the fabric industry, but the car was there. "So you bought a sports car?" Jenny laughed at the ridiculousness of the vehicle for the Midwest winter weather, but everyone got to make their own choices.

Mickey turned back to look at the car. "You think I bought it? Oh, gosh, no. I just rented nicer than economy for the first time in my life."

Jenny nodded. "Now that I understand. How fun to enjoy it for the weekend. Be careful, though. These roads get slick in this weather."

"My mother said the same thing. But . . ." Mickey did a little spin, losing a red card from her pocket in the process. The snow fell lightly on her skin, and she looked radiantly happy. "I love it! I don't get near enough of this in Tennessee."

Jenny bent to pick up Mickey's stray card. There was no envelope on it, but the front looked hand-painted. It was a modern Christmas mantel with a pile of folded quilts in a basket next to a blazing fire.

"Here, you dropped this."

Mickey looked at it and cringed. "Just toss it. Do you mind?"

Jenny looked down at the card and back at Mickey. "Why would you toss it? It's beautiful."

"Only the outside. The message is totally creepy." She waved at Jenny, brushing the idea away. "You can read it if you want."

Jenny opened the card. She read the message and immediately looked back at Mickey.

Mickey raised an eyebrow and nodded as if she was looking at it with Jenny. "See what I mean. I don't want that around."

Jenny looked back down and read the whole message again, slowly. It was written in verse, a parody to the familiar Christmas carol "Deck the Halls" but with an ominous change to the lyrics.

Deck the halls with bows of folly,
Fa la la la la, la la la la.
Time to purge designer dollies,
Fa la la la la, la la la la.
Your playtime game of lies is severed,
Fa la la, la la la, la la la.
Tell truth or lose what you most treasure.
Fa la la la la, la la la la!

"What is it talking about? A game of lies? Is something going on?" The note was not only creepy, but threatening.

"Not that I know of. I'm just trying to make fabric

and help my family out. I can't tell you what good timing it was to finally sell a fabric line."

"You're not worried about this?" Jenny asked, holding the card out to return it to Mickey. She held her hands up and stepped back to the car.

"I don't want it. There's nothing I can do about it anyway. Just toss it." She shook her head, rolling her eyes. "I knew becoming a designer would change things, but we haven't even announced my line yet. Someone gave me this in the airport." She shook her head.

"Who?" Jenny was shocked that anyone would just hand this kind of note over to its intended recipient.

"Just an employee. They called my name while I was waiting on luggage. I opened it in the car. Super weird, right?"

"Mickey!" Tilly called from the doorway. She and Maura hurried down, greeting Mickey with hugs all around.

Jenny looked at the card and tucked it into her pocket, but she couldn't help worrying. Why would someone be so bold about a lie Mickey apparently knew nothing about?

Cherry joined Jenny and the chattering girls on the lawn as Mickey pulled out luggage and a stack of boxes from the back seat of her fancy car. A horn honked, and another car's window rolled down as it pulled up in front of the house.

"I told you we should have carpooled." Helen Derrick leaned out the window, waving at the women huddled together on the lawn.

"Looks like the gang's all here," Jenny said as Helen parked the car and jumped out to join them. Her deep purple jacket over fitted jeans almost matched Mickey's purple sweater and gloves.

"I guess the rest of us didn't get the memo," Jenny pointed out the matching outfits.

Helen and Mickey laughed like teenagers.

"I swear we don't do this on purpose," Helen said, making the rounds with hugs for each of them.

"It happens at least once at every retreat, though," Tilly teased.

Mickey shrugged, a grin on her face that echoed the feeling in Jenny's heart.

"It's so good to have you all here," Jenny said to the circle of women.

"It is." Helen squeezed Mickey on one side of her and Maura on the other. "Because I have a ton of luggage."

More laughter circled the group and Mickey concurred, waving Tilly and Maura to her car while Cherry joined Jenny and Helen to help her unload.

Helen unloaded more bags onto the sidewalk than anyone had brought yet. Jenny took two and looked at Helen as she closed the trunk. "You know you're only here for a week, right?"

"Hey, I didn't want to limit myself. If I start getting a lot done, I'll need options. Only one of these is clothes, the rest are projects. Mickey and I are working on matching wall hangings. And this one is the quilt I promised to bring."

They moved everything inside, and Jenny thrilled to see her friends and their bright smiles together again. It was all the confirmation she needed. This was going to be a wonderful retreat.

Applause rang through the theater as Jenny finished her welcome spiel. The crowd was entirely fabric industry professionals, and Ron stood beside her on the stage as they shared in their excitement for the coming week.

"I am so thrilled to be able to say I already know many of you, and I can't wait to get to know the rest as we go through this week together. We'll get to introduce your new fabric lines to the quilting community, win over new customers, and hopefully make a lot of new friends! What do you say?"

Cheers resonated through the room and Jenny raised her hands in the air. "Let's meet some of the company heads that are making this week possible."

Colored lights flashed on stage like they were at a dance party. Standing in the wings was a line of fabric manufacturers, including Sally Harper and her co-owner, Owen Teak. The two had their heads together, talking animatedly under the music playing through the overhead speakers. As the announcer called out names, the line got shorter. When they got to Harper Wovens, the pause was evident. Someone had to give the two company

14

owners a push before they realized they were late.

Owen came out waving, with a huge smile on his face, and the crowd laughed. He gave Sally a twirl, but when they passed Jenny, his smile seemed strained. Once the other designers were called and they were excused, Owen was the first one off the stage.

The whole welcome wasn't long, but Jenny couldn't focus through the last stretch. Ron even had to prod her to wave when it was over. She hurried offstage into the building filling quickly with designers and manufacturers, but Sally and Owen had disappeared.

Several big names like Vana Suze with her manufacturer stood at the stairs, and a new designer, wearing a dress entirely made of half square triangles, twirled in the lobby. A well known manufacturer chatted happily with Lizzy Rose, one of Harper Wovens' top designers. He slipped her a card, and Lizzy hesitated before taking it. Jenny wondered briefly if Lizzy was looking to switch companies.

Before she could go up and talk to her, Hugo Hensen pushed past toward the door.

"Excuse me," Jenny said, moving out of the way as quickly as she could.

Hugo didn't seem to notice. He only spared her a glance before pushing out into the parking lot.

Sally hurried after him, only to return a moment later, worry lines pinching her forehead.

"Sally? Is everything all right?" Jenny looked

out the glass doors where Sally had followed Hugo. She couldn't see anything but the reflection of the party. "Is Hugo upset?"

"He's always upset," Sally said absently. Then she seemed to come back to herself and smiled up at Jenny. "He's been collaborating with us for awhile, and sometimes he's just like that. Don't mind him. That was quite a show, Mrs. Jenny Doan."

Jenny smiled, but bypassed the compliment. "Sally, I can tell you're worried about something. What's going on?"

Sally bit her lip and rubbed hard against the fingers of one hand with the other, her eyes darting around the room. They finally landed back on Jenny. "Owen's worried about Mickey. And now Hugo being like this. I don't know what to do."

"Can I help? Is it about the note Mickey got earlier? I'd be happy to talk to her. Do you think we should we call the police?" Jenny was trying to remember if she'd put the note in her purse or left it at home when she realized how confused Sally looked.

Her brow had furrowed and she had cocked her head, her mouth open like she was waiting to speak. "What note? Mickey just hasn't picked up our calls yet and I haven't seen her yet. I figured it was Mickey being a diva . . . is there something we need to worry about?"

Jenny had been spending far too much time worrying about this.

"Maybe." Jenny had never considered Mickey to be anything other than polite but Sally had called her a diva almost like it was a given. "I'll talk to Mickey when I see her."

"Well, hopefully you'll have better luck than us. We can't find her."

2

"Mickey doesn't want to be bothered. Trust me." Helen laid out her bundle of red and white fabrics and pulled out an extra fabric bin she'd tucked under her table.

It was the morning after the welcome event. Everyone but Mickey was sitting at their sewing tables or snacking on brunch foods Cherry had brought. It was the second time Jenny had come by, only to find Mickey was once again unavailable. She'd tried to see her on the way home from last night's event, and this morning she'd expected to be able to talk to her when she'd arrived. Apparently, Mickey was too busy.

Jenny leaned into her table, pinching the red and white fabric block she was putting together and whispered to Helen at the neighboring table. "But she missed the entire Welcome Night. Why would she skip her first big designers event? Not even Sally knew where she was."

"Why do you think I would know?" Helen

asked, the irritation heavy in her voice. "We had an argument. Then she left. I thought she went to the big fancy designers thing."

Jenny paused, realization dawning. Helen was jealous. Jenny could understand that. It was great to see a friend do well, but when it was something she'd always wanted as well, there was bound to be a little jealousy.

The note Mickey had received was tucked under the edge of Jenny's sewing machine. It might explain why Mickey was on edge and fighting with people, but not why she refused to take it seriously. Jenny was planning to call the police about it if Mickey didn't, just to be safe.

"When did she get home?" Jenny tried to keep her voice down. She didn't want to bring the whole room into her concerns.

Helen shrugged, and flipped through the pages of a pattern before setting it back down.

"Did you hear her come back?" Jenny had to remind herself not to be frustrated. It wasn't Helen's fault Mickey was acting unreasonably.

Helen didn't answer for a moment. Then she looked up at Jenny. "I heard her come in. She didn't get back till around midnight. So I'm sure she's sleeping in."

Jenny glanced at Mickey's empty sewing table and pursed her lips. "You're right. I'll give her some time."

Helen rolled her eyes. Her attitude toward Mickey had done a one-eighty from the day before.

A Body in Redwork

Jenny took a deep breath, turning back to the rest of the room. She needed a distraction.

"Does everyone have a plan for their red and whites?" Jenny asked the room at large.

"Summer in the Park," Maura called out, naming one of Jenny's earlier patterns.

"Ooo, I love that one. You can call it Holidays in the Park," Tilly said, laying out fabric on the cutting mat. "I'm making 'Handy Dandy.' It's been on my list since it came out, and I think this will be perfect for it." She had to push aside a small Christmas tree she'd brought with her to make room for the fabric. She didn't seem to mind. In fact, her whole table was decorated in glittery garland and snowflakes, with a tiny fabric poinsettia flanking the tree.

"What are you making?" Bernie asked Jenny.

She picked up her fabric bundle and tried to visualize what she was going to be making. A red and white star quilt. She'd been working on the pattern for months, just letting it percolate in the back of her mind while other things required more attention.

"I'm making a lemoyne star for Santa Claus." She grinned and set the fabric in the middle of her table.

There was a whole stack of blocks in various stages of production scattered across the surface. Several looked finished, while others were the bare beginnings of a star, and still others had been completely ripped out. "I'm filming the lemoyne star soon, and this is going to go with the Mr. and Mrs. Claus outfits Ron and I have. We're going to ride in the parade on Sunday."

"That's adorable." Tilly put a hand on her hip and looked at Jenny with something akin to envy. "Someday I want to be you. Can I do that?"

"You don't need to," Jenny responded. "You are perfectly adorable already."

She looked around the room at the happy women. Aside from Helen everyone seemed to be enjoying themselves. She hoped she'd be able to keep that feeling going all week. It was a lot of pressure, but with two assistants, it shouldn't be a problem. "How about you, Bernie?"

Bernie adjusted her glasses and rubbed the bridge of her nose. It was a funny little twitch, but when she lifted and released her shoulders, her expression changed to a self-satisfied grin.

"I have no idea." Bernie settled back in her chair. "I'm waiting for inspiration to strike me."

Dotty tossed a wad of batting over their machines, landing it right on her sister's chest. The two were the only locals at the retreat beside Jenny and Cherry. Their constant banter and playfulness made it easy to forget they were easily the oldest of the crew.

"Hey, that doesn't count!" Bernie's long silver braid swept around her shoulders as she twisted away from the white fluffy batting, snatching it back up at the last minute. "But if you're ready for a snowball fight, so am I."

"Snowball fight at the end." Jenny couldn't help the smile on her face now. "Your snowballs can only be made from batting cut from the projects you make this week."

Laughter and chatter filled the room as the women worked faster. The front door creaked, announcing a visitor had arrived.

"Someone has got to oil that door." Maura waved a thin ruler toward the entry. "It was going all night."

"Yeah," Tilly said. "Who's the party animal? I just left a house where very small people were waking me up at all hours of the night. I was hoping for a good night's sleep."

The door closed, and Andi Grant walked in, a large box of garlands and ribbons in her arms. Her dark hair was wrapped up tightly in a woven scarf with just a few corkscrew curls escaping the edges of the bright fabric.

"Hi, Jenny," she said cheerfully. "I hope everyone's having a good time. I brought decorations!" She dropped the box onto the couch, the sound of jingling bells giving away more of the contents.

"Nice to see you Andi. We don't need all of that, do we?"

Cherry leaned forward, watching Andi while trying to put a pin in the nearby pincushion . . . upside down. She dropped it when she stabbed her finger. "Ow."

Andi came over with a fist full of red berries and

23

sat down next to Jenny. "I hope you don't mind that I took the initiative to make things a little more cheerful in here. I know you like it when people make things happen. If you give me a few minutes, I'll get the decor set up, and then I'll get out of your way. Let me know if you need anything, won't you?"

"Jenny was just saying she wished she had a list of the upcoming projects for the week," Cherry said, referencing a question Jenny hadn't even thought to ask. But Cherry was right; it would be nice to have a list.

"I sent decorative lists for everyone and coordinating patterns in the boxes that Hugo delivered yesterday," Andi responded confidently. "Did you miss them?"

"Hugo was here?" Maura perked up, scooting her chair out and getting stuck on her sewing machine cable at the same time. She blushed but didn't take her eyes off Andi.

Cherry's hand came up to stop Maura. "No, actually, he wasn't here. Sally Harper delivered supplies. It's really important to keep track of who's doing what when handling things for Jenny."

Jenny couldn't understand what had bothered Cherry so much that she'd started being rude to Andi. It was like she felt challenged or misplaced.

"Sally Harper was here?" Tilly squeaked. She took a step closer, knocking the edge of her snowflake garland off the table and leaving it puddled on the floor.

Andi smiled at Tilly. "I have connections. We can talk later if you'd like to meet her."

Cherry crossed her arms, disguising the wedding ring quilt pattern that suffused today's sunset-colored blouse. "How is the food being handled?"

"Catered by Poppy's," Andi said without missing a beat. "She's making lemon poppy seed cake for dessert today. That's your favorite, isn't it, Ms. Carmine?"

"Poppy seed?"

Cherry's voice perked up, and Jenny forced down the laugh that bubbled up in response to her friend's sudden excitement. Maybe it was all in her head. But Cherry's smile dropped, and she shot Jenny a glare before turning back to Andi. "I mean, that's nice. What about tickets to the events?"

"Already booked." Andi's smile grew tight, but she didn't back away.

Cherry's eyes narrowed, and she leaned forward as if she was in an assistants' duel, facing off over the living room settee and firing questions like ammunition. "Even the trade show?"

Jenny wasn't sure this was going to end well.

"Done," Andi shot back. She took a step toward the box of Christmas decorations and pointed at them as her way of asking permission. "I'm going to get decorating now. If that's all right."

It wasn't really a question, and Jenny's quiet laughter at the two women's battle for dominance earned her a smack on the shoulder.

"Don't you laugh at me. I heard she's gunning

for my job." Cherry watched Andi carry a child-sized Christmas tree to the parlor.

"Who told you that? She's an artist. If anything, she wants a job with the design team."

"And working for you wouldn't look good on her resume at all," Cherry snapped back. "Sorry. I know I'm overreacting. But she came by after you left yesterday. She made a show in front of the girls about being glad she could help you since everything was too much for me." Cherry's normally cheerful face was pinched and focused on Andi as she tipped the box of decorations onto the couch. "And now she's doing it again. I'll try to chill out."

"Nobody sit for a while," Andi said. "Except you Cherry. I can tell you're still injured, just do it over there please." Andi indicated the parlor across from the dining room and Cherry's jaw tensed.

"Oh, she didn't." Cherry stood and walked away from Jenny, reaching for a strand of garland. "Here, let me help you."

"No!" The annoyance in Andi's voice amplified along with its volume, and she grabbed the garland before Cherry could even touch it.

The outburst drew the attention of every woman in the room. Sewing machines slowed, and all eyes turned to Andi, who chuckled nervously and patted the greenery in its spot. "I just mean, I already have a plan. You don't need to worry about it."

Cherry raised an eyebrow and pasted on one of the fakest smiles Jenny had ever seen. "Tell me the plan."

A Body in Redwork

She lifted the garland, and Andi gripped it again. Both women stared at each other, in a silent tug of war.

Slowly Andi's lips turned up into a mildly sinister smile. "I don't think that's necessary. I'll be fast. Then I'm off to take care of a few more things while you sew. There's really no need to feel threatened."

"I don't." Cherry scoffed and let go of the garland. Andi didn't stumble but you could see the pressure release when she stepped back. "I'm going to finish what I'm doing. You finish your stuff. That's a beautiful bracelet, by the way."

The bracelet was unique with tiny dance shoes, a painter's palette, and a circular charm painted with yellow enamel. The whole thing looked familiar, but Jenny couldn't place it. Andi pulled her sleeve down and walked away with the garland in hand.

"I'm sorry. I'm trying to be nice," Cherry whispered.

"You really don't have anything to worry about," Jenny said.

"I know I don't, but it feels like she's declared war," Cherry said as Andi strung garland and ornaments up over doorways.

"A war of Christmas decorations?" Jenny shook her head. "Just don't break anything, okay?"

"If I decided to play her game, there wouldn't be any question who'd win." The intensity of Cherry's gaze made Jenny laugh again.

"What?" Cherry asked indignantly, shoving

Jenny's shoulder. "I'm trying to be serious here. No laughing."

"I'm sorry," Jenny said, focusing on her work. "Just tell me when the dust settles."

"I see you doubting me. It's fine. I don't mind. I'll deal with this situation on my own." Cherry stood and started back to her sewing table, chin held high.

While Andi strung garland over doorways, Tilly had the instruction page open for one of the supplied projects. Both Bernie and Dotty were working on a little pincushion at a table on their own wall of the living area and Maura was slicing through a set of fat quarters.

"Anyone know what Mickey brought for presents this year?" Maura paused after cutting her fabric and looked up. "You don't think she brought us new fabric from her line, do you?"

Dotty set a completed pincushion down on the table. "No idea. But it's nice to see someone we know living her dreams."

It was silly, but Jenny had the inclination to raise her hand and point out that many of them were also living their dreams. They just might not have turned out to be as glamorous as Mickey's.

Maura pulled a set of fabric strips through her machine. "I can't believe she's Harper Wovens' newest designer. She's famous!"

"She's not famous. Yet," Tilly corrected, acting as the resident Mickey Stevens expert. She paused a moment, and then her smile spread, lifting her cheeks to rosy apples. "But I bet she's going to be!"

28

A Body in Redwork

Maura stopped sewing, her fabric strips still pinned under her sewing machine's presser foot. "Do you think she'd teach me what to do so Harpers would notice me?"

Helen's expression soured, her lips turned down and her eyes narrowed. The other women didn't seem to notice.

Maura dug into her gift bag and pulled out a brand new stack of fabric from her favorite designer. "If anyone gets famous enough to meet Hugo Hensen, you have to bring me with you."

"Maybe that's what Mickey is bringing for presents this year," Tilly teased. "A designer crush for everyone!"

"Mickey doesn't always have to be the center of attention." Helen shot the words out as if she had no control over them. She slammed a sketch book closed and marched out of the room, leaving the women silent.

Andi stepped over, her gaze darting to the doorway where Helen had gone. "I think I've got the decorations up. I'm heading over to the Sewing Center. I have to catch up on a couple things with the event team."

"Of course. Thanks for your help." Jenny caught Cherry pursing her lips and ushered Andi to the door.

"I can be back this evening to help with things. Food, or activities. I did towels and a few sheets last night, so you should be good on laundry, but I'm happy to help."

Andi's chipper willingness seemed to eat at Cherry's good graces from across the room. Jenny opened the door for Andi.

"I think we'll be fine, but thank you again. I'll let you know if I need anything else." Jenny shut the door behind her.

Cherry stepped up next to her. "If she's too busy at the Sewing Center I can take over. I'm feeling fine."

"That won't leave you much time for sewing." Jenny pointed out.

Cherry let out a breath. "I know." She lowered her voice and leaned in close. "I just don't like the way she takes over."

"Who's that?" Maura asked, pointing out the front window.

Bernie lowered her glasses as a blond man in a brown coat passed the window. "Why do you want to know?"

"He's handsome," Maura said admiringly. "And he's been by our window half a dozen times now."

Bernie snickered. "Hands off, ladies. That's our local police officer. Besides, if anything ever happens to Stewart, he's mine."

Cherry choked on her water, and laughter erupted around the room. Stewart was Bernie's husband and while she knew there was no truth in the statement, she couldn't help laughing. Jenny joined Maura, looking out the window.

"What is a police officer doing in front of our window?" Helen had reappeared and stepped up to the window beside them, arms folded, watching the man pace outside.

Officer Wilkins paused and looked at the front porch. He turned away, then pivoted, walking toward them again.

Jenny excused herself and pulled the creaky door open. The officer stopped, eyes wide when Jenny appeared on the porch. "Officer Wilkins, it's good to see you."

"Mrs. Doan," he blurted. He jumped up the steps onto the porch, tripping when he finally made it to the top. "I was, uh, looking for you. And please, call me Tyler. I'm off today, so it's just plain-clothes Tyler."

"Well, come on in, Plain Clothes Tyler." Jenny held the door open for him.

"Tyler?" Cherry asked from behind Jenny.

"Yes ma'am," he replied, a deep shade of pink growing on his cheeks.

Cherry shifted her weight and frowned. "I was expecting Frank or Travis or some other tough guy name."

He furrowed his brow. "You don't think Tyler sounds tough?" His voice dropped a level, deepening the tone.

"You're the toughest police officer I know." Jenny led the way into the main sewing area. Tilly had disappeared, but everyone else had gone back to sewing as if they hadn't been watching the officer through the front window moments before.

He followed her in and shook his coat off,

rubbing warmth into his bare fingers. "Ron told me you would be here for a while, and I have a question for you."

"Well, I have a question for you, too." The note under the edge of her sewing machine burned bright red. She picked it up and turned back to the officer but she hesitated giving it to him with the way he watched Cherry. Jenny had the sneaking suspicion the officer wasn't there to talk to Jenny at all. Of course, ever since Cherry had rescued the young officer, he'd started turning up everywhere they went. "Come on, Tyler. Let's be honest. Is it me you'd like to talk to or Cherry?"

Tyler's cheeks bypassed every other shade of pink and went scarlet red. He ran a hand through his hair and looked at Cherry. "I, uh, wanted to . ."

It was like his words literally stuck in his throat.

"What did you want?" Cherry asked as Jenny sat back, thoroughly entertained by the two of them.

"Some help coming up with a gift for my mother."

"Your mother?" Cherry asked.

He nodded, and Jenny let out a breath. "Your mother?"

He turned to face Jenny, suddenly looking about ten times more comfortable. "Yes. I want to make her something."

He glanced at Cherry.

"All right. What were you thinking?" Jenny wanted to shake him. "Since you're here, I assume you mean you want to sew her something?" She wondered if that would make him nervous, but he nodded. She invited him over to sit in the chair next to hers.

Cherry pulled up the Missouri Star Quilt Company website and selected the appropriate tab for beginner projects. "Look through here. Let me know if you find anything your mother would like."

He started scrolling through the site, every few seconds tracking Cherry across the room while she wandered around talking to people and surreptitiously adjusted the decorations Andi had put up.

Jenny shook her head and grabbed a spool of thread on her sewing table. If he wasn't going to fess up to the real reason he'd come, Jenny didn't feel so bad bringing him work on his day off.

She pulled the card from her pocket. The next time he paused, Jenny leaned forward and handed him the card. "What do you make of this? My friend Mickey received it yesterday."

"What is it?" he asked, raising an eyebrow as he took the card.

"Read it," she said simply. Truthfully, she didn't have anything else to tell him. She was more confused by it than anything.

He was silent for a moment and then looked up, his brow furrowed. "That is strange. Is there any context?"

Jenny shook her head and rubbed a chill from her arms. "Not that I know of. One of the strangest parts is that she received it at the airport. Someone knew her plans well enough to leave it for her."

Tyler rubbed at his jaw. "Do you think I could talk to her?"

"Mickey?" Jenny looked up the stairs, tapping a spool of thread absently against the table. "I think she's still sleeping."

He handed the card back as footsteps pounded down the hall overhead.

"Help!" a voice called from upstairs.

Tyler was instantly on his feet.

Tilly grabbed the rail at the top of the stairwell, swinging her body to a stop. Her face was as pale as if she'd seen a ghost, her blond hair lit from behind and glowing as if she were one.

"Jenny. Officer. Somebody, help! I think Mickey's dead!"

3

"Where is she?"

Officer Wilkins bolted up the stairs, taking them two at a time without any issue. Jenny followed him, catching Tilly at the top. She was breathing fast, tears streaming down her cheeks.

Tilly pointed to the only open door in the hall: Mickey and Helen's room. Her hand dug through her hair and clutched her head like she was trying to hold her mind inside her body.

"I didn't know it was her. I thought it was a pile of laundry. I was looking for Mickey, then I saw her in the blankets. She didn't move, so I tried to shake her. I was worried she'd fallen off the bed and hurt herself . . . , I just wanted to wake her up, but she was so cold."

Jenny looked back at Mickey's open door.

"Can I go?" Tilly's small voice had flipped from the yelling and panic of a moment before. Her trembling hands echoed her distress. When Wilkins nodded, she gripped the railing and ran down the stairs.

Officer Wilkins held a finger to his lips and started slowly to the open door. The words of the Christmas carol rang in Jenny's head. *Deck the halls with boughs of folly*. A shiver ran down her spine, knowing she was likely going to see what it meant.

Officer Wilkins disappeared on the other side of the door. Jenny hesitated, waiting to see if he would reappear, but the hall stayed empty. The need to know finally pulled Jenny forward.

She swung the door back to see Wilkins kneeling over a large redwork quilt rolled haphazardly on the floor at the end of the bed. For a moment, Jenny didn't notice anything wrong. Then she saw a hand peeking out from the edge of the blanket and a section of the tell-tale red hair dangling onto the floor.

"Mickey." Jenny breathed her name and dropped to the ground beside the quilt.

Officer Wilkins only looked up for a moment. "This is a crime scene. Be careful."

"She's really dead?" Jenny's throat tightened. Up until that moment, she hadn't been sure, like maybe Wilkins would come back saying everything was fine.

In answer to Jenny's question, he pulled a fold of the blanket back so Jenny could see what he was looking at.

Mickey was painted like a giant doll.

Her skin had turned waxy white against the bright colors of the makeup. A black line had been drawn above and below her eyes like stitches, and large pink circles sat high on her cheeks. Her lips were bright red, so solid it didn't look like lipstick anymore.

Jenny couldn't breathe. Her hand came to her mouth and a gasp of disbelief squeaked from her as she caught the reality of what she was seeing. Mickey was dead.

"I, uh, I'm going to go back downstairs. I think I need to—" She stood and stepped back to the hallway.

"Wait. Mrs. Doan. I need you to stay close." Officer Wilkins—she couldn't think of him as Tyler when he was kneeling over Mickey —Officer Wilkins gestured for her to follow him as he went back into the hallway. "Stay here, please."

Wilkins crept down the hallway and slipped into the next room. Jenny could still hear her friends whispering downstairs, and someone was crying. Jenny still hadn't figured out how to get her lungs working smoothly. She leaned back against the wall, trying to breathe.

The person on the floor didn't even look like Mickey. What was she going to do? How was she going to tell Mickey's family? Was that her job?

Jenny turned back and looked into the room. Mickey's pale form lay still on the ground. Jenny tried to look over her and see what she'd missed the first time, but a sob caught in her throat. This was her friend.

Wilkins made his way through the last of the bedrooms before heading downstairs. Thankfully,

37

he beckoned her to follow him.

She hurried behind him and made her way to the huddle of friends surrounding Tilly, who was the one Jenny had heard sobbing.

"Is it true?" Maura still had a pattern book in her hands; her fists were clenched around the pages, wrinkling them in her grip. "Is Mickey really dead?"

Officer Wilkins had disappeared into one of the side rooms. Jenny looked back to her friends. There wasn't any other answer. She nodded, and gasps sounded through the group.

Jenny could feel her own lip quiver as Tilly began to cry harder. Helen's hands trembled and breathed the word, "No," shaking her head.

Cherry was the only one who hadn't really known Mickey and even she stared openly at the stairs in a state of shock.

By the time Officer Wilkins returned the women were a mass of tears and sniffling. They'd asked repeatedly what had happened and Jenny could only confirm over and over that she knew nothing.

Wilkins held a phone to his ear, his voice low. "Yes, Berry Street. Send a team. One dead and . . ." Wilkins hesitated and Jenny looked up meeting his gaze. He looked away. "Seven suspects."

Jenny's blood went cold. Of course they were suspects. She looked around at her traumatized friends and hugged as many as she could get her arms around.

"It's going to be okay."

A Body in Redwork

Officers hummed around the rooms, taking pictures and examining everything. The women hadn't been able to let go of each other the entire time. When Jenny had left to answer the door, arms had closed the gap she left, supporting each other from all sides. And when she'd returned they'd opened again without question, letting her slip into their borders of comfort and strength.

That is, until the police officers had arrived. There were several officers now and they'd started taking the women aside individually. The small group had dwindled to only a few and as the hours ticked by, Jenny and her friends started to separate and rest, forming smaller clusters on the couches or in the outlying rooms. Somehow the large dining room had become too close to their loss.

Jenny found herself in the kitchen. The cider was still boiling but the scent of soap fought for dominance as she scrubbed the dishes in front of her. Cherry dried and spoke quietly about what they were going to do.

Tilly leaned against the counter watching. "I already called the airline. I hope that's okay. I figured I had better check, but they said I can switch my flight to as soon as tomorrow. Do you think that will be okay?"

"Jenny?" The deep voice startled them. Officer

Wilkins stood still in his plain clothes, though now with a gun harness strapped around his shoulders and a walkie-talkie on his hip. "I need you to come with me."

"Of course." The feeling in the room had already been sober, but as Jenny left Cherry and Tilly, a dark gloom seemed to rest behind her, compounded by the unsolved problems and worry in their eyes.

He circled the dining room looking for a quiet place and finally moved toward the stairs. "Would you mind if we do this up here? We'll have a little more privacy."

Jenny didn't respond, just nodded and looked up the stairs. He led her to a corner on the main landing away from the bedrooms, a slightly quieter spot. "Tell me what you remember about the last time you saw Michelle Stevens."

Jenny opened her mouth and looked down the hall where a set of police officers discussed something quietly. The red notecard was now plastic-wrapped and in one officer's hand. She tried not to think about it's threatening message or her friend in the far room. "Not much. The last time I saw Mickey was yesterday morning and afternoon. Everything was good. The girls and I were all happy to see each other, we visited, and then I left to go to the first night of the designers convention. Mickey was supposed to be there too."

"Was she?"

Jenny shook her head. "No. Sally said she wasn't picking up her calls though. She didn't seem

40

worried or anything. She just kept saying it was normal. Owen seemed worried about her." Jenny still couldn't imagine Mickey playing the diva like Sally had said but something had to be off. She had been killed.

"Who are Owen and Sally?"

"The owners of Harper Wovens, the fabric company that hired Mickey recently. Do you think that's what it meant in the poem? When it said *time to purge designer dollies*? Mickey was a brand new designer and you saw how they dressed her. Is someone killing designers?"

Officer Wilkins raised his eyebrow at her. "Do any of your guests paint? Or have access to paints?"

"No. It's a quilt retreat." Jenny paused and looked down the hall. "Except, well, Helen paints."

Jenny remembered the solid red lips and nearly choked. "Was that really paint on Mickey? Someone painted her?"

"I didn't say that." Officer Wilkins raised an eyebrow at her.

"But she was. Painted, I mean. Her lips were so red. I assumed it was makeup. Who kills someone and then paints them?"

Wilkins ignored her comment. "You said Helen paints?"

"Yes. But she doesn't kill people. She's an artist. Before Mickey was signed, Helen was working with her to try and get fabric lines picked up together." Jenny shook her head. "But I'm sure she keeps her paints put away."

"What does that mean? Get fabric lines picked up?"

"That's when an artist or designer takes their ideas and images to the fabric manufacturer and tries to get them to turn their work into fabric. They usually only do one or two lines per designer each year, and each company can only take on so many designers. It's a pretty big deal when you get chosen as a new designer. Mickey was so excited. It kind of makes you a superstar of the fabric world."

Wilkins raised an eyebrow. "So someone might get jealous if they felt someone else had been 'chosen' when they should have?"

Jenny knew what he was implying, but it made her sick to think about it.

"You can't mean Helen," Jenny defended. "Maybe someone got her paints, but she couldn't do that."

"She could if she had the right tools," Officer Wilkins said as he made more notes.

"Then she wouldn't," Jenny insisted, hoping her glare would help him see how serious she was.

Wilkins didn't respond, just moved on to more questions. "Did anyone know which room was Mickey's?"

"All of us did." She threw her hands in the air, rolling her eyes. "Are you going to accuse us as a group?"

Officer Wilkins simply waited.

"You're infuriating," she said, folding her arms.

"That's my job," he muttered, and looked up with a gentle smile.

A Body in Redwork

"We all helped her and Helen unload and get settled in. They picked the biggest room 'cause they both brought so much stuff."

"Helen shared a room with her?"

Jenny nodded.

"Is there any reason she might have chosen to stay in another room last night?"

"Excuse me?" Jenny had come in early that day but Helen. . . Where had Helen been? In her mind's eye, Jenny could see the room behind Mickey. One of the beds had been entirely rumpled and unmade while the other had been pristine as if it hadn't been slept in. Of course, Helen had switched rooms. "Helen and Mickey argued. She must have gotten pretty upset if she switched rooms."

"What did they argue about?"

"I don't know."

"When did they argue?"

"Yesterday?" Jenny said it like a question, still trying to remember. "Yeah, Helen said she fought with her and then Mickey went out."

Wilkins nodded and something dropped in Mickey's room. He turned and something else fell. "Shoot. Can you wait here?"

Wilkins disappeared down the hall and a few seconds later was walking someone with an open box held between them away and down the stairs. "I'll be right back," Wilkins called to her.

Jenny turned around the landing and waited. The police officers that had been discussing Mickey's notecard had disappeared as well. Jenny moved to the hallway and glanced behind her. Officer Wilkins was still gone. She wanted to help Mickey. It seemed impossible that she was really there in the bedroom, dead. She took a few more steps this time prepared for what she was going to see.

Mickey's body had been uncovered with little numbered markers scattered around. One sat on the redwork quilt that had been folded next to Mickey's body. The red stars were staggered between solid red blocks with a tiny bit of stitching in the corners. It was beautiful, similar to what she'd planned to make with her redwork blocks. Another tag sat next to a red scarf. Jenny looked down at Mickey and closed her eyes immediately, turning away.

She looked at the quilt again. The familiarity let her relax. Stitches and fabric were far less intimidating. On the quilt were two red cards. Jenny squinted and took a step closer.

One was certainly the notecard Mickey had received the other day, but the second was new. They were both wrapped in plastic and she pulled out her phone trying to zoom in on the image. She took a step closer.

"Mrs. Doan?" A police officer stationed in the room identified her by name. "Can I help you?"

Jenny didn't flinch. "Oh, no. I was just getting a picture of these cards for Officer Wilkins. I'll just be one second." She took a quick step and snapped a picture.

"I don't think you're supposed to be here." He

44

crossed the room hesitantly as if trying to decide if he should believe her.

"No, it's fine. I'll just be one more . . ." She flipped the bagged cards over. They were open so you could see inside them while they were in the evidence bags and snapped another picture. "There. All done."

She hurried out of the room, pausing and turning at the doorway. This time she intentionally looked at Mickey. Her friend was gone. The body that lay there was painted and different but she still wore her designer's pin.

"Did you get lost?" Wilkins' voice grabbed her attention and Jenny moved to meet him.

"Mickey was planning to attend the welcome event."

"Why do you say that?" Wilkins asked ushering her back into the open landing area.

"Because she's wearing her pin."

The officer looked at her blankly and Jenny made a gesture to her own shirt in the spot where Mickey's pin would have been attached. "Her designer's pin. Harper Wovens gives them to all their designers to be worn at public events. It helps people know who's who, with so many groups. And Harpers is the only company that does it. It's like wearing a gold medal when you walk around with a Harper Wovens pin on your chest. Last night would have been Mickey's first opportunity to wear hers."

"Oh." He looked back to the room and nodded.

Jenny waited while he made a note. "Was Mickey strangled?"

The question was blunt and the words hurt slightly, but she wanted to know. Wilkins didn't answer and Jenny wasn't surprised. "I saw the marks on her neck and the scarf, and maybe I'm jumping to conclusions, but that's why I'm asking you."

Wilkins took a deep breath, "That's what it appears to be. Some twisted person snuck in here, killed her, then painted her up like a cartoon."

"Not a cartoon, a dolly." Jenny could see the words of the threatening card Mickey had received. *Time to purge designer dollies.* "I should have never invited her." Jenny looked away, her stomach turning. "I should have canceled the retreat. I should never have invited any of them."

"This isn't your fault." Wilkins transitioned back to business. "Whoever killed Mickey came into her room in the middle of the night and strangled her with a scarf. Did you let them in?"

Jenny shook her head.

"Did you threaten Mickey with creepy Christmas lyrics?" Wilkins looked her in the eye.

Jenny shook her head.

"Did you provide the scarf or anything else?" He didn't even wait for her to deny it. "Of course not. We're going to figure this out. Leave it to us, and you take care of the rest of your guests. Okay?"

"I can do that."

A Body in Redwork

The doorbell rang on the main floor. Jenny turned. "Speaking of guests, I should probably go see who that is."

She was grateful for the officer's good intentions, and prayed that he was right. She needed them to figure out what had happened. As she walked away, her fingers itched to look at the pictures she'd taken, but below her the door creaked open again. She hurried down the steps.

Helen stood by the entry next to Lizzy Rose. Another member of the Harper Wovens team. She looked like a vintage movie star with her dark hair and red lipstick. She wore a gray scarf and long black jacket, and, with the exception of her lips, she looked like she'd stepped out of a black and white movie.

"You don't understand." Helen was saying. "Mickey's not here because she died last night."

Lizzy's mouth dropped open as Jenny arrived. "Liz, I'm so sorry you had to find out like this." Jenny could feel the strain of politeness as she tried to help her unexpected visitor. "Is there something you needed?"

"Mickey," she responded, with wide eyes. "I was supposed to get Mickey."

Jenny didn't know what to say. Helen sucked in a breath and Lizzy reached out. "I'm sorry. I'm so sorry. I had no idea."

She was obviously trying to be sensitive, and Jenny stood awkwardly as Lizzy hugged Helen.

When she stepped away Lizzy took a ragged

breath and shook her head. "When did . . . it happen?"

"Last night." Jenny said. "Or this morning. We're not sure."

"Okay, well, I should probably go. I'm only in the way here." Lizzy took a backwards step and Helen grabbed her arm.

"But don't you want to talk to someone? They're taking statements from everyone who saw her." Helen's brow was furrowed and Jenny took a second look at Lizzy's wide eyed innocence.

"Did you see Mickey yesterday?" Jenny couldn't understand why she'd be lying about seeing her unless she had something to hide.

"Oh. Not really. I came by to help Helen feel better after Mickey made her feel bad, but it was nothing."

Helen shook her head and started to say something else when Lizzy reached out, taking Helen's shoulder. "If you think I need to tell them about my little visit, I can do that."

Lizzy smiled widely then tamed it into something more respectable for the death of a friend.

Jenny watched her walk away with Helen. The two of them argued quietly. The interaction was strange but when Cherry walked up she tried to let it go.

"Are you doing alright?" Cherry asked, putting an arm around her.

Jenny breathed out and hugged her friend back.

"I'm fine. I'm just confused by this whole thing. Mickey was a good person. I know good people die but not like this."

Cherry pulled back and looked at Jenny. "All kinds of bad things can happen, even to good people."

Jenny nodded and pulled her phone from her pocket. "I know, but I just don't understand. Look at this . . ." She opened her camera screen. "They seemed to think she was a liar."

Jenny zoomed in on the image of the notecard and paused. The image she'd pulled up wasn't the first notecard but the second. She scanned the words, and realized it was the second verse of the poem Mickey had been threatened with before she'd died.

Fast away Ms. Stevens passes.
Fa la la la la, la la la la.
Hail! She stole from honest lasses.
Fa la la la la, la la la la.
Strike the Harp she's left the chorus,
Fa la la, fa la la, la la lu.
A fabric of lies she's left before us.
Fa la la la la, la la lu la.

4

"What kind of lies do they think she was telling?" Cherry whispered harshly. "Was Mickey a thief?"

Jenny read the note again and furrowed her brow. "Surely not. But whoever killed her seems to think she was."

"Cherry, Jenny." Officer Wilkins approached with his notebook in hand and looking unexpectedly intimidating with his shoulder holster visible. "Everything all right?"

"We're fine," Jenny said.

At the same time, Cherry said, "Are we safe?"

Wilkins brows went up and he looked between the women for a moment.

"*Hail, she stole from honest lasses,*" Cherry repeated. "If Mickey stole something that led to her death, we need to know what it was. Or else we could all be at risk."

"Oh." Wilkins looked at Jenny who grinned sheepishly and tucked her phone away.

The police officer adjusted his holster. "We honestly don't know. Hopefully, this won't ever happen again. As terrible as it is, my hope would be that Mickey did something worth killing her for, and we never hear from this guy again."

"Mickey didn't deserve to die," Jenny said emphatically. "Even if she lied or stole. She didn't deserve to die."

"That's true. But it still happened."

Cherry made a worried squeak. "I haven't been lying, I don't think." Her voice wavered slightly as she thought back. "That's what the killer seems to be upset about right? So if I didn't steal or—"

"Cherry, you'll be fine." Jenny said, pulling up her phone. "See in the first poem they referenced *designer* dollies. You're not a designer."

Wilkins broke in. "You should still keep your eyes open. Be safe. Whoever did this committed a clearly thought-out murder. It wasn't an accident, and you can't assume you're safe because of a line from a poem."

Cherry's face was pale and she had a hand over her mouth.

"You've been so helpful, Officer Wilkins," Jenny said. "Can I talk to you?"

"Of course." He said, and after reassuring that Cherry would be alright, Jenny led him away to the kitchen.

"You've got to be more careful with these women," Jenny said, looking back toward the doorway that led to the rest of the house. "They're not all going to be responsive to that much openness."

"And what do you propose? That we put blinders on them? Say go do whatever you want, a killer's on the loose? Watch out for people with paintbrushes." Wilkins' tone grew intense, matching Jenny's.

"No. But I don't think it's necessary to put every woman in town in a state of panic when his notes indicate some specifics about people who should be worried."

"Uh huh." Wilkins dug a hand into his hair and reeled back. "Notes, as in information you shouldn't have, and I don't want to know how you got it."

"Do you want to know what I think?" Jenny held up her screen, displaying the image of the note.

Wilkins threw his hands up and walked away only to turn back again, hands on his hips. "Sure, Jenny. You might as well tell me what you think."

Jenny pursed her lips and let out a breath before turning back to the screen and jumping in. "The killer referenced *designer dollies*, right? And *a fabric of lies*." Jenny flipped between the two poems. "Even the line about the harp. Harp is capitalized out of place, and Mickey worked for Harper Wovens. This all seems hyper focused on the fabric world, in particular: Harpers. But the fabric and design world is so small. If her stealing something was the trigger, I can't imagine how she could get away with it."

"I'm not sure she did get away with it." Wilkins looked at Jenny's phone and reached over, flipping the image to the second poem. "*Strike the Harp*, huh? I'll think about that. Be careful, Mrs. Doan. I know you feel like you've done this before, but murderers don't care if you have a job and a family at home when you get in their way."

Jenny leaned against the counter as she watched him go, then flipped the light off. She could feel tears filling her eyes again. The dark room gave her a moment to feel just a little bit invisible.

Someone shuffled to a stop outside the kitchen door, and Jenny took a cleansing breath to compose herself. If she was going to see people, she needed to be calm. Then they spoke, and she froze.

"I understand you shared a room with Mickey?"

It was a police officer she didn't recognize and she was over hearing his session with Helen.

54

"Yes." Helen's solemn tone hurt Jenny's heart. She wanted to go wrap her friend in a hug, but if she came out and Wilkins found out she'd overheard even part of the conversation, he'd have another reason to be upset with her.

"Can you tell me why you decided to switch rooms last night?" To the officer's credit, he asked the question gently. She was grateful he wasn't steamrolling her like it was an interrogation.

"We had an argument. Mickey didn't want to share the room with me anymore." Helen sniffled after her blunt answer. The clipped words were low and steeped with emotion. "I tried to show her some of my recent work and she got upset. She was better than me, and she wanted to make sure I knew it. So I took my pillow and I left. That's the last time I saw her."

Jenny covered her mouth and kept still. That interaction didn't sound anything like what she would have expected. No wonder Helen hadn't wanted to talk about it.

"And you went to Ms. Walker's room? At what time?"

"Ms. Walker? You mean Tilly?" Helen asked. "Eight. But Mickey came home around midnight."

"How do you know that if you were in Tilly's room?" the officer asked, focusing his fingers on typing out what she was saying.

"The front door is noisy. You probably noticed."

Jenny realized she was biting her lip and had to force herself to relax as the officer asked his next question.

"Did anyone come in with her?"

"I don't know." Helen's voice cracked. She was crying. "I put a pillow over my head and tried not to think terrible things about her."

"So you don't really know if that's when Mickey came in or if someone was with her or if it was even her at all."

Helen sniffled and it took her a moment to calm down. Her next words were quiet. "She was alone. At least for a minute. I looked out the door and tried to talk to her. She ignored me." She stopped talking again, and the officer waited. "That's when I put the pillow over my head. I didn't want to think about how she was being so hateful. Lizzy tried to tell me what Mickey was like. I just couldn't see it before last night."

"Lizzy? Was she there last night?"

More quiet. Helen must have nodded because the officer spoke again.

"When was Lizzy with you?"

"She came around six. Shortly after Jenny left. And again, around ten. We had an argument with

Mickey and she left. That's when Tilly came upstairs."

"I thought you said Mickey didn't get home until midnight."

"She didn't, but she didn't leave the house until ten after Lizzy and I argued with her."

"So you saw Mickey at six, ten, and midnight. And what did you argue about?"

A pen was scratching away and Jenny sidestepped slightly to see if she could get a view of what was happening.

"Fabric. Her line, my art. There was a lot of comparing and accusations. Lizzy didn't believe Mickey and it wasn't very friendly."

Jenny's throat went dry. She could picture the officer nodding or raising an eyebrow or wearing any number of expressions. What she couldn't imagine was why Helen hadn't mentioned that to her earlier. She thought Helen would have trusted her.

"How does Lizzy, or Ms. Rose, know Mickey?" he asked.

"Mickey and I were both in her fabric design class a year ago. We thought it would be fun. Liz stayed in touch with all of us. She wanted to help us out."

"And that's why she came over? To help you out? Why not just get rid of Mickey? That would open a spot for you to become a designer, too, wouldn't it?"

"No!" Helen sounded panicked. "You don't have to kill someone to become a designer. These are good people. And I didn't hurt Mickey. Liz was just trying to help me feel better, and Mickey was being very hurtful. I told Liz about it and she came over. She brought a book of all the new fabrics to show me. It was supposed to be exciting . . ." Her voice trembled, its tone implying anything but excitement.

The kitchen door opened. Jenny held her breath. She was going to be caught.

Andi came in, a stack of papers in her hand, and Jenny almost closed her eyes for half a second, hoping it would hide her.

"Jenny!" Andi never seemed to notice or care when Jenny acted strange. "I forgot to leave these with you earlier. They're the patterns you need for tomorrow."

"Hi, Andi." Jenny stepped forward and took the patterns from her. In the corner of her eye, Jenny saw the officer scan the kitchen and scoot Helen away. Jenny let out a breath like she'd had her lungs in a vice grip.

Andi glanced at the hallway, thenback at Jenny. "I'm sorry, am I interrupting something?"

Jenny almost laughed. It was more than a little

relieving to not hide anymore. "It's fine. Thanks for bringing the patterns. I'll hand them off to Cherry in a little bit, if that's all right."

"Oh, no problem," Andi said, completely distracted by the hustle and bustle of the room. "Did something happen? Why are the police still here?"

Jenny looked down, struggling with the words. "After you left, we found Mickey Stevens in her room. She died last night."

Shock tore across Andi's face as her mouth dropped open and her eyes grew wide. "Like a heart attack? There was so much yelling last night. I wish I'd known she had a problem."

"Someone was yelling?" Jenny asked. Andi nodded.

"Yeah, Helen and Mickey were going at it." Andi's brow pinched. "I could imagine someone's heart going out after that kind of stress."

"No . . . it wasn't an accident, either. She was killed." Saying it still left a bitter taste on Jenny's tongue. "The police are trying to figure things out, so they're taking statements. I'd forgotten you were here. You should stay and talk to them?"

"I don't think I'd be very helpful. I mean, I heard Helen and Lizzy Rose and Mickey arguing, but I'm sure others did too." Andi looked over her shoulder, and her voice dropped to a whisper. "They were fighting pretty bad. You don't think one of them killed her, do you?"

"Well, I didn't." Jenny hesitated. She was starting to reconfigure the event in her head. "Would that have been during the Welcome event? I've been trying to figure out why Mickey would miss it."

"It could have been." Andi's eyebrows rose, and she leaned in conspiratorially. "I had to leave early, around six-ish, to go help with the event, but they were just getting started."

"Do you know what they were fighting about?" Jenny whispered.

Andi shrugged and looked around the room as if trying to find the answer. "Something about fabric. Mickey did something they didn't like."

They. Jenny considered her words carefully. "Would you be willing to talk to the police about all that?"

"Of course." Andi reached a hand up to her throat nervously but smiled, her charm bracelet dangling off her arm. The yellow circle Jenny had noticed before hung at the bottom of the chain.

The charm flipped around, and the familiarity clicked into place. It was a replica of the Harper Wovens pins. "Oh, where did you get this? It's exactly like the designer pins."

Andi looked down and almost jumped when she

realized what Jenny was talking about. "Oh, you know. Get to know the teams and you get great swag." She pulled her sleeve down again. "I have to get going. Can you tell Officer Wilkins that I'll be in touch about a statement?"

Cherry walked in as Andi was pulling the door closed. "Now you're meeting with her in secret?"

Cherry's tone was teasing and Jenny rolled her eyes. "You know it's not like that."

Cherry went to the back door, checking that it was really closed. "I still don't like her."

"You like everyone," Jenny reminded her.

Cherry harrumphed and turned away from the door. "I know. And she is very helpful, so, it's making this really hard."

H elen's canvas leaned against the headboard of her bed, a large drop cloth covering the bedding. Brushes lay scattered on the nightstand with a smear of paint still on the palette.

It was Tilly's room. The same one where Helen had stayed the night before. Jenny moved closer to the canvas. The bright colors were reminiscent of the notes Mickey had received, but the technique was different.

"What are you doing here?" Helen appeared in the doorway drying her hands.

Jenny turned, trying not to bother any of the supplies she'd been examining. "I wanted to check on you." She paused, and Helen brushed past her, taking one of her brushes and sweeping up a dip of red paint. Jenny tried again. "How are you doing? I know you were close friends with Mickey for a long time."

"Not as close of friends as I thought." Helen stroked the paint over a quilt scape that Jenny suspected would turn into a quilt hanging on a clothesline. With its sunshine and green grass, it was completely unlike the winter landscape outside. Even in the beginning stages of the artwork, it felt like an escape.

"I tried to go into our room. I wanted to see Mickey. I guess the authorities didn't like that idea." She looked blankly toward the door behind Jenny, then turned haunted eyes on her and shook her head. "There's so much I should have said. How was I supposed to know it would be the last time I saw her?"

"No one can know that. Not when it's like this." Jenny's heart ached for the loss of their friend and the pain the rest of them were going through.

Helen looked away and slashed her paint brush

over the canvas, red paint bleeding across the gentle scene. "I don't know how to be okay. The last thing I said to her was that I never wanted to see her again. But I didn't mean it. I just want to talk to her. Ask her questions. I want my grandma's quilt."

Jenny pulled back at the shift in the conversation. She didn't understand why she was worried about the quilt when Mickey had died, but she tried to be sensitive. "I'd forgotten you were bringing a quilt to share." Jenny's mind flashed to the redwork wrapped around Mickey's body. "It was your grandmother's redwork?"

Helen smiled slightly "All red and white stars and hand stitching."

Jenny didn't want to say it but she didn't want Helen to find out through a careless word from a police officer. "I think your quilt is going to be tied up in the investigation for a while. But hopefully not too long. I'm sure you'll get it back soon."

She could feel the lie in her words and she bit back the grimace. She had no idea how long the quilt would be gone, but Helen needed reassurance.

Even that wasn't enough. Helen's smile dropped. "What do you mean? It's my grandmother's redwork quilt. It's not part of an investigation. It's a family heirloom."

"You're right, of course, but Mickey was, well,

Mickey was wrapped in your quilt when we found her. So, it's part of the evidence now. It's going to be a bit before you can get it back."

"What?" Helen's cheeks paled, her eyes as wide as unsewn yo-yo plates.

Jenny cringed. "I'm sorry, Helen. I wish there was something I could do."

Helen sucked in a startling breath. She suddenly looked near tears. "It's not your fault, and it's not even the quilt. I'm sorry." Helen started putting her brushes and paints away, indiscriminate of what the tools were or where they belonged. She sniffled and gave a vague glance around the room. "Can you give me a minute?"

"Sure." Jenny gave Helen a quick hug and left the room, not sure if she'd done more harm than good.

In the main living area downstairs, Officer Wilkins cleared his throat. "Excuse me, ladies. I want to say this to everyone at once. I've heard a few people talking about changing flights or trying to get home. While I recognize you may be personally struggling after the death of a friend, I have to remind you that you need to stay here until we can determine what happened."

Murmurs spread through the little crowd. Some had hands to their mouths or open shock on their faces as Officer Wilkins motioned to his partner and started for the door.

"Does that mean you think one of us did it? Because Helen was the one yelling at her and I was in bed when people were coming in last night," Maura said, stopping the young officer in his tracks.

Several women gasped and Maura flinched. She knew she'd been too harsh.

Officer Wilkins looked around at the distressed women. "I appreciate your situation, but that's not something I can say at this time. Keep an eye out for each other. This is going to be a stressful time for everyone. And while I don't intend to detain you, it would be to your benefit if you would cooperate."

Silence fell over the room, and Jenny hurried down the stairs, following the officers onto the front porch. "Wait. Tyler? I mean, Officer Wilkins. They really can't go home?"

He sighed and looked behind her, where the news of their imprisonment was not going over well. "I know it's not easy, but there's no sign of forced entry. It looks like it happened late at night while the other women were sleeping in the home." Officer Wilkins' voice lowered with every sentence. What he was insinuating wasn't good. "I'm sorry, Jenny, but these women are our prime suspects."

Jenny was shocked. What would she do with eight

women who were all terrified one of them was a murderer?

Seven.

The weight of Mickey's loss hit her once again. Only seven women, including herself. And they were all hurting. "You can't do this to these women. You can't force them to stay here, where Mickey was killed." Jenny couldn't seem to keep the intensity out of her voice, even at a whisper.

Wilkins didn't look happy, but he scrubbed at his jaw before making up his mind. "Then get them hotel rooms," he said, "because they can't leave town."

5

Jenny and Cherry spent all day trying to find anywhere in town that still had rooms to host half a dozen women for the week. When Andi called to tell them she'd found a solution, they were both grateful. But, as Cherry's little red convertible pulled up in front of the large brick building, Jenny's morale dropped even further.

"We can't stay here," Jenny said. They were parked in front of the Missouri Star Quilt Company's Sewing Center.

Several signs announced the opening of the designers convention that would be held in the Sewing Center's main hall on Thursday and Friday. Until then, the entire thing was being kept under wraps. The windows of the lower level had even been blacked out, concealed by large curtains and hung with homemade Christmas decor. All along the street, the large windows sported beautiful holiday vignettes with a large tree as the corner window show piece. There was nowhere for a group of eight women to live for the next six days.

"You said she's on the event team, right? She should know it's booked." Cherry shook her head as she cut the engine, her eyes on the building.

Jenny nodded and pulled open the door. Andi stood on the raised sidewalk in front of the Sewing Center, wrapped in a coat and lemon-yellow scarf, rubbing her arms in the cold.

"What's the plan?" Jenny called cheerfully, trying to catch the young woman's attention as she and Cherry made their way up the steps to meet her.

"This is it!" Andi waved a hand overhead, indicating the very unavailable venue they'd been discussing.

"You're kidding." It was Cherry's southern accent that conveyed both their shock.

"I understand your concern, but listen to this." Andi glanced at Cherry but otherwise stayed focused on Jenny. "I talked to the other coordinators, and since we only need a few of the upstairs rooms for storage purposes, they have agreed to let us use half the rooms above the convention."

"Seriously?" Jenny shot a glance at Cherry. "We'll take it if that's true."

Cherry grudgingly agreed it was a good idea, and Andi gave a little cheer before hurrying off to finalize the details.

"Let's go upstairs," Cherry urged after Andi disappeared. "I want to see if there's anything I need to take care of up there." Cherry got more excited with every step. "I'll be able to decorate this entire place."

"It already has decorations. You don't need to do anything." Jenny's mind was plenty full with worries about friends and the investigation. She didn't need to stress over making an already beautiful building prettier.

"I'm going to decorate it." Cherry dismissed Jenny's comment with the wave of her hand. "Andi's busy with the convention downstairs. I don't want her to feel like she needs to do this too."

"We actually don't need it," Jenny said as she turned into one of the bedrooms. "Besides, if we really want Christmas decorations, I'm sure Andi would bring her garlands and bells up here."

"I'd like to do this." Cherry stopped when Jenny raised an eyebrow at her. "Okay, yes. I want to make sure Andi doesn't try to one up me here, too. But I also need a distraction right now, and the girls will need something to lift their spirits. Just let me put up some pretty things. It's going to be beautiful."

"Fine. That makes sense but I don't like to see my assistants battling over something so silly."

"It's not a battle. It's war." Cherry lifted a shoulder and leaned her head into another room. Jenny couldn't help laughing to herself. Cherry never lacked for sass.

The bedrooms had tall ceilings and two, three, even four beds. White walls and vintage sewing finds sat on the nightstands. The fluffy bedspreads echoed the light, bright feel. Mostly it was lovely and easy.

The upstairs of the Sewing Center had been designed with bedrooms on either side of one long hallway between two sets of stairs. One set of stairs led to the main floor at the back end of the hall, and the other set of stairs led directly to the sidewalk through a private entrance on the other end of the hall, where Cherry and Jenny had just come up.

"Do you want to go down?" Jenny asked when they reached the open stairwell at the other end of the hall.

"Hmm?" Cherry asked, her eyes on the long white hall behind them. Visions of sugar plums surely danced across the moldings in her mind. "Oh, no, that's alright. I'm going to work on some ideas. Let me know if you need anything."

Without another glance, Cherry headed back

down the hall, muttering to herself and running a hand along a feature or light fixture as she passed them. Whatever this little competition was in Cherry's head, Jenny hoped it didn't cause her any trouble.

The designers convention hall was actually the main hall of the Sewing Center. Transformed to highlight multiple fabric companies and individual designers, the entire floor had been sectioned off into a large grid of metal poles. As she descended the stairs, she could almost see the whole thing. Square booth sections lined the walls with single and double wide compartments across the floor. Unfortunately, the base of the steps was almost blocked by the back of one of the booths that had begun setup.

Jenny stepped off the grand staircase and came face to face with the back of a booth circled in bright jewel-toned fabrics. She slipped past the draped walls and found herself in a multicolored box. Across the booth Jenny recognized the tall figure and blonde waves of Sally Harper.

It was a double booth with walls made of tone-on-tone prints designed to echo regency brocade. The walls moved in a rainbow of shades. Only about half of the fabric panels were hung from the metal poles, but the colors ranged from hot pink to deep navy and lilac. Stacks of ivory fabric dress forms lay in one corner of the booth behind a large, multi-armed chandelier. Its long arms were wrapped in a bright floral fabric resting precariously on a small carved settee covered in ivory to match the dress forms.

Sally was supervising someone carrying a ladder. Her hair was tied up in a ponytail, and she'd traded dress slacks for jeans. She once again had a large box in her arms while she directed the ladder to the center of the room. When they set it down, Jenny realized Owen had been carrying the ladder. He grabbed hold of the large chandelier as Sally climbed up on the first rung.

"Owen! I need—oh!" Sally wobbled slightly but got herself back in control as Owen handed the chandelier up to her. He stayed below, balancing the arms, and together they hefted it onto a support hook.

"Good work! This place is going to be beautiful!" Jenny encouraged the pair. "I didn't think anyone would be setting up yet, but you guys are almost done!"

"I wish we were that close." Owen traded places with Sally and started wrapping the base of the decorative fixture onto the crisscrossing framework. "Sally has way too many plans for this place. We had to start early."

A Body in Redwork

Sally lifted her eyebrows and grinned up at Owen. The two had been partners from the very beginning, and while they'd always gotten along, Jenny had never heard about a relationship beyond that. They worked well together, though.

"Well." Jenny looked around. "What can I do to help?"

Owen gave Jenny a look as he picked up two dress forms at once. "Oh, be careful what you ask for. The designers aren't coming in until tonight before the Q&A, and some of them aren't picking up calls still." He paused, his brow pinching just slightly as he shot a quick look at Sally, before turning back to Jenny with a grin. "So if you ask to help, you will be used."

Jenny pushed her sleeves up. "Give me a job."

It wasn't long before Jenny was hanging drapery across the walls while Owen set up dress forms and Sally dressed them. By the time they were done, it would resemble a ballroom.

"You know, once upon a time I thought I would be a fabric designer. I'm not an artist, though." Jenny shrugged.

"If you ever want to give it a shot, I'd love to chat." Sally leaned out from the hot pink mannequin, a huge box of safety pins in her hand and several between her teeth. The cotton ball gown had a full skirt and a string of buttons down the side of the dress.

Jenny tried not to let the comment sink in. "That ship set sail and cruised into the sunset without me. I've got plenty to do anyway." She was well aware that designing wasn't in her wheelhouse, and letting that idea settle wouldn't work out well. "You've got some amazing designers on your lineup. You don't need me."

"You'd be surprised," Owen mumbled as he set a naked dress form in front of the green panel Jenny was hanging.

Jenny watched him walk away, wondering if he knew she'd heard the comment. Both the owners seemed focused and she realized neither of them had mentioned the repercussions of losing Mickey.

"We always need good people. Like any business. And especially in the fabric industry. Trends are fickle." Sally pinned the arms of the dress in place and fluffed the skirt before she looked up. "If Mickey's line lives up to the hype, things will finally start looking up, I think."

"Do you think it will be alright after all? You know, now that Mickey is gone?" Jenny tried to broach the subject delicately.

Sally huffed around the half dozen pins pinched in her mouth and pulled them out to reply. "I know we get frustrated, but she's not really gone. She's pretty good at dodging calls, but she'll get here."

"Wait. Lizzy didn't tell you?"

Sally looked up from her work and Owen stopped cold. The sound of emptiness echoed at a disturbing level.

Jenny took a slow breath, still shaping the words. "At some point last night—" her words failed her, mouth dry.

Sally's brow furrowed, and Owen stepped out from behind the dress dummy.

Jenny swallowed and tried again. "Mickey was killed last night."

Sally's entire box of pins dropped to the ground with a sound like tiny shattered bells. They scattered over several booths until the quiet engulfed them. Between the three of them, it felt like Jenny might be the only one breathing. Owen looked at Sally.

"I just thought she wasn't answering. That she was being a diva again," Sally said to no one.

"I'm so sorry," Jenny started, but Sally shook her head and put her hand to her mouth.

"What are we going to do? I can't believe she's gone." She wobbled, and Owen abandoned the dress forms as he ran to catch Sally before she fell.

He helped her to the couch, and Jenny found her a water bottle.

Sally's eyes were clear now, but her brow had furrowed tightly like she was nursing a headache.

"I know this is a hard time to ask but you said Mickey was a diva. Did that create problems with the other designers? Was there anyone that would have wanted to hurt Mickey?" Jenny looked between the two of them as more footsteps sounded through the empty hall.

Sally shook her head. "Not really. Everyone knew it but as far as I knew they just ignored her and left it to me."

"You weren't the only one that Mickey treated like that, but it wasn't her nature." Owen shook his head. "It happens a lot with new designers. Typically it's one of two responses. They come in acting like they're no one or like they're here to save you."

The footsteps stopped and Owen looked up to greet whoever had arrived.

Jenny turned and Officer Wilkins stood behind her. "Well, how nice. It looks like we have a mutual friend."

Jenny tipped her head and looked back at Sally. "I guess so. I've known Sally and Owen for a while. I can introduce you or I can give you a little space."

"Space would be great, thanks." Wilkins stepped forward not waiting for anyone to object. "Hello,

Ms. Harper and Mr. Teak?"

They nodded and Jenny excused herself through the front door onto the sidewalk. She pulled her coat tighter in the cold. It wasn't snowing today, though remnants of white remained on the railings and benches. It smelled like pastries, and Jenny considered going into the bakery for a cup of peppermint tea before Cherry opened the door that led out from the upstairs.

"Jenny?" She sidled up next to her, rubbing her gloved hands together. "What are we looking at?"

"The snow, the town. Thinking about going back and gathering up the girls so no one has to stay at the house."

"I already called Bernie and Dotty. They're getting everyone together as we speak. I think we can expect them within the hour."

"Will they even have clothes?" Jenny couldn't know what the police would let them remove and she felt terrible about everything. "We can't let this keep going. Someone has to find this person."

"The police are doing that." Cherry reminded her but Jenny shook her head.

"The police are following my lead. I told them about the connection to Harpers and after I go talk to them Wilkins shows up. I know he's a great guy and even a great police officer, I just feel like I need to find out what really happened."

Cherry clasped her hands and leaned onto the railing. "This is important. I can understand why you're worried."

"Thanks, Cherry. Do you have big plans for the new retreat location?" She tried to lighten her words though the heaviness of Mickey's death didn't change.

A tiny smile appeared on Cherry's face. "They're coming together. I actually need to head home. Are you ready to go?"

"I think I'm going to stay out for a bit. Maybe get some tea." The conversation she'd had with Owen and Sally was circling in Jenny's head. "I can walk home or call Ron if I need to."

Cherry said goodbye and left quickly while Jenny crossed the street to the bakery. The tea smelled wonderful, the mint and sweetness mingling together. Jenny held her hands against the warmth of her cup and sat at the side window. The side of the Sewing Center loomed next to her and Jenny sipped at her tea. Owen had seemed more sympathetic to Mickey than even Jenny had been feeling after hearing Helen's arguments and finding out the side of her that Sally had known.

While she hated to think it, Helen had the most evidence against her . . . And opportunity. She'd been alone with Mickey several times through the night. And Sally; what good would it do for Sally to kill off one of her designers? None as far as Jenny could tell.

Across the street there was a movement in the alley behind the Sewing Center. Sally was leaning against the building with a hand on her head and her eyes closed. Jenny hopped up from her table and, grabbing her tea, hurried across the street.

"Sally," Jenny called as her friend started to retreat behind the building. "Sally, can I talk to you?"

Sally turned her mouth open in surprise. "Jenny? Hi. I thought you had left."

"I did. Just to get some tea. I needed a break." She held up her cup and slowed her pace to match Sally's.

"I can understand that. I really can't believe Mickey died. We had a lot of plans with her. She was doing a lot. When we hired Mickey, she had a lot of big ideas, but she was . . . demanding," Sally paused and looked up with a sad smile. "We didn't get along well."

"Nobody's perfect." Jenny commiserated with Sally as they walked. They stopped near the back of the building where a small deck had been built to access the alley. Sally put her hand on the railing but didn't go up. "Mickey probably stepped on a few toes with her attitude."

Sally's eyebrow lifted and she stifled a grin. "Nobody's perfect," she reiterated, then looked up at the door to the building. She looked like she didn't want to go. "She didn't get along with very many people in the company. Of course, she was perfect to her fans," Sally said. "She had quite an online presence."

"That must have been appealing when she came on. It's hard to build a following."

"Honestly?" Sally looked around verifying they were alone. "I thought she was going to save Harpers. Shoot us back into the mainstream of trendy design. Now, it feels like every other attempt we've made. Plug the money in and then watch it go down the drain. We don't even have a designer for the new organic fabrics division she was spearheading."

"I didn't know you were starting a new fabric division." Jenny knew how great a new division like that could do if they hit the right market, but without anyone to lead it, they'd be back to square one searching for the right design match.

"It was Mickey's idea. Of course, she was doing the main fabric lines. You know, if she hurt anyone, it was Lizzy and Hugo. They were working on additional lines for the organics but she didn't want

80

either of them there. She was a diva. There's just not much way to say it besides that." Sally took a couple steps and turned around. "You know what else? Lizzy was instrumental in her getting hired. She'd advocated for her, and then Mickey turns around and treats her like trash. I just don't understand some people. She played with emotions and loyalties like toys and then tossed them away when they weren't useful anymore."

Sally was halfway up the stairs now. Her hand had started to tremble. "I just want to be clear, we wanted Mickey to work for us. We used to be a team. But she made her own enemies."

It only took a few hours for the women to gather their things and fill in the space over the Sewing Center. And by the next morning they had pushed beds back in the largest corner room, turning it into a gathering space.

Maura, Tilly, and Helen had settled what they had of their things in the three person bedroom. Bernie's sewing machine was the only one humming. Jenny sat quietly in one of the chairs they'd placed in the corner room listening to the quiet start and stop of the vintage Singer.

Jenny was supposed to be filming a lemoyne star block at the end of the week, but she hadn't worked on it since they'd found Mickey the day before.

Dotty had begun a sampler of blocks by Hugo Hensen; Helen sat on one of the beds; Tilly was in the hall on the phone. The somber feeling that permeated the rooms was so different from the day they'd arrived. The memory made her cringe, a surreal mix of pain and disbelief.

When Tilly returned, she flashed a bingo card at Maura. "I just got three designers who came in the wrong door and I had to redirect them."

Bernie laughed, and a feeling of uncertainty filled the room. How could they laugh when their friend was gone?

Maura frowned at Tilly. "No, you didn't."

Tilly laid her card out in front of Maura. "Vana Suze, Sylvie Sweets, and Maggie."

"Who's Maggie?" Maura went digging for her own card. "I know all the designers on my card."

Andi had printed bingo games of the designers at the beginning of the week, adding a little fun to the retreat. Jenny hadn't thought anyone would pull them out now, but the friendly competition could prove to be a fun distraction.

Tilly shrugged. "I don't know. She works for a new company called Pears & Gin, but she's on my card." Tilly waved the partially filled card at Maura.

Maura found a pen and searched her own page. "Fine, then I get Lizzy Rose. I answered the door for her . . . yesterday."

And just like that, things sobered. Remembering what had happened yesterday was enough.

A knock sounded at the door, and Officer Wilkins leaned his head in. "Jenny? Can we ask you a couple questions?"

"Oh, yeah." Tilly blushed and gestured to the officers. "The police are here. They wanted to talk to you."

Jenny jumped up. "Of course. I'll come out."

She joined them in the small hallway where they were waiting in full uniform.

"Good morning, Mrs. Doan. We wanted to ask you a couple of questions."

"Of course, anything you need." Jenny clasped her hands in front of her.

Wilkins pulled his notepad out. "We always appreciate your cooperation. First, I wanted to see if there is anyone else that may have had access to the house?"

Jenny hesitated. "I don't think so. Andi only gave the code to the retreat guests. I can't think of anyone else, except, well, Sally Harper was there that morning, delivering boxes for Andi. She had the code too, but that's all."

Hillary Doan Sperry

"Liz." Helen's voice was small behind her. Jenny turned to see her friend standing in the doorway to the corner room. "Lizzy Rose had the code. I gave it to her so she could visit."

Officer Wilkins scribbled a few notes down. "That's good to know. That relates to the second thing. We're looking for Ms. Rose. Do either of you know where we can find her?"

Jenny pinched the corner of her shirt hem and shook her head. "The last place I saw her was at the retreat house."

The officers thanked her and walked away. Jenny turned to Helen. Her eyes were dark, and her skin was pale and bruised like she'd been crying.

"Are you going to be alright?" Jenny asked gently.

Helen's lip trembled. She tipped her head into a slow back and forth denial. "I don't think so. Jenny, I don't know if anyone else knows it, but Liz was there that night. We fought with Mickey. We had a good reason, but we fought."

"What happened?" Jenny looked down the hall, wondering if she should call the police officers back.

"Mickey's new fabric line." Helen looked away. "It's from my art. She stole my line."

84

6

"I know, I don't have a fabric line, so can I even be upset? But she stole my work." Helen repeated the accusation like she was reaffirming the validity of her claim. Her eyes shifted to the window as if she could pretend she wasn't admitting this to anyone. "I didn't think it was good enough. Then she found my preliminaries and sold it to Harpers."

"Are you sure? Maybe she just did something similar." Jenny didn't mean to doubt her, but the idea that Mickey could steal an entire line of artwork was unthinkable.

Helen looked broken, like the life had been sucked out of her. "Oh, it's similar alright. So similar that my signature is still in the teacups."

"No… Mickey?" Jenny wanted to offer an explanation, but she didn't have one.

Helen's eyes glistened with tears. "I was always

so proud of her. I would have been first in line to support her. Buying her fabric, talking her up."

"What happened?"

Helen opened up like she'd been waiting for someone to ask. "Liz found out. She was showing me the new Harper Wovens fabric book, and there it was. We confronted Mickey. That's why we were fighting. And she acted like it was nothing. I mean, it's true that I'd thrown it out, but that doesn't make it hers. She can't do that." Helen trembled as if going into shock. "Mickey wanted to get picked up as much as I did, but she wouldn't even apologize. I wasn't going to say anything about it to the police. I don't know how it can help anyone to know Mickey did something so terrible, but I've been sick over it."

"Of course." Jenny wrapped her arms around Helen. She patted her shoulders and tightened the embrace when Helen started to cry.

"I didn't know she was going to die," Helen sobbed.

"Of course not," Jenny comforted. "We're going to figure it out. It's going to be okay."

It's going to be okay, she repeated in her mind. They would find whoever did this and it would be better. The police emerged at the other end of the hall. Helen's head was bent, still crying, and Jenny leaned low to get in her view and reclaim her attention.

"I know this is hard, but Officer Wilkins is right down there. You should tell them what you told me. I don't know if it will make a difference, but they need all the details."

Helen nodded and made her way down the hall.

Tilly leaned out the door. "Is Helen okay?"

Jenny wasn't sure, but she nodded anyway. "She'll be fine. She's struggling with Mickey's death. Sally was having a hard time, too."

"Really?" Tilly asked, "I didn't think they got along very well."

Jenny's brow furrowed. She looked at Tilly. "That's what I learned today. Sally was calling her a diva. I should probably go talk to her again."

"Yeah, this is going to be rough on Harpers." Tilly stepped out into the hallway and shut the door behind her. "From what I've heard, they've made some sketchy financial decisions lately. Owen talked about Mickey's line like it was going to save them. I assume they'll still be able to print it, but one line versus a successful designer is nothing."

"They're struggling financially? Where did you hear that?"

Tilly shrugged. "I don't remember, online somewhere. I follow almost as many designers as

Maura. It's kind of fun to see what everyone is up to. I've just seen some comments on posts and such. It's not gospel or anything, but when a story repeats, it usually has some truth."

Tilly watched Helen with the police officers for a moment, then turned. "Are you coming in?"

"No. I need to straighten some things out." The truth of Mickey's death felt convoluted. She was wrapped up in secrets and a life her friends had never known about. Jenny tried to think it through, but there were too many moving parts. She needed to be able to visualize them all together.

Across the hall, Jenny opened the door to the last room of the retreat. They'd stacked all their extra storage things to save on space in the other rooms. Jenny scanned the bins and large bags of fabric and found her design board tucked into a corner, along with a bag of her extra quilt blocks. She had planned to make a sampler quilt with them, but they would fit her purpose for now.

She emptied the bag of blocks and spread them out on the table. Picking up a small brightly colored pinwheel, Jenny marked it with a scrap of paper labeled 'Mickey' and pinned it to the center of the design board. An hourglass block was the next one on the stack. Jenny picked it up.

"Who are you?" she asked, turning the creamy

yellow and blue block in her hands. Who would want Mickey dead? In a quick realization, she labeled the block "Sally" and pinned it next to Mickey's block. Jenny laid a small sashing strip between them and labeled it "stolen fabric line." She placed a cornerstone piece up with "diva" written across it and another labeled "struggling company."

But Sally wasn't the only person with animosity toward Mickey. She pulled a soft green and purple churn dash from the pile and labeled it "Helen." She pinned it on the board with a sashing that said "fight with Mickey."

Jenny leaned back and considered the pieces at play. She grabbed a couple more quilt blocks and set them back down when several spools of thread tumbled out of the bag. She grabbed one. She turned it on its end, unspooled a stretch of it, and wound it back up.

Lizzy Rose should probably be on there, too. Jenny knew the police had been looking for her, though she didn't know why except for her confrontation with Mickey. For the sake of being thorough, she pinned a dark blue and cream nine patch near the top of Mickey's block.

She turned the spool of thread in her hand. It was a deep gray. She tugged at the end, tightening it as she turned it over and around. She stared at the board. Jenny knew everyone on there, and her heart stung with every name. She kept twisting the thread, trying to see who would have done this. Jenny reached out, taking the "stolen fabric line" sashing from between Sally and Mickey and moved it to lie between Mickey and Helen. That was better. Mickey had stolen the fabric from Helen, but it left an empty space between Sally and Mickey.

The cornerstones were there. Jenny knew Sally's company was not doing well. The pin was a question, but she still had to determine if there was a more direct tie to Sally than that. There were a lot of questions still. A messy patchwork of questions. And very few answers.

Jenny couldn't see any pattern to it. She pinned up a few more pieces but couldn't decide where they fit. She labeled a sashing as "red scarf," the murder weapon. To a dark cornerstone block, she added, "door code."

"I'm not sure I'd want to make that quilt."

Jenny smiled without looking at the newcomer. She knew Cherry's voice well.

"This isn't a quilt that anyone wants until it's done." She looked at her friend. "And then they'd only want to put it away."

90

A Body in Redwork

"What does the 'door code' block mean?" Cherry said, coming into the little room and picking through Jenny's quilt blocks.

"Whoever came in had to either be let in or have a code, and none of the girls said they let anyone in, or were even awake at the time. So this goes by the people who had a door code to the retreat house."

"But it's just sitting out here in the middle of nowhere." Cherry picked up the corner and let it flop down against the board.

Jenny raised an eyebrow and removed the block. "That's because I don't know who to put it by. Both Lizzy and Sally had the code."

"Hmm. Well, who's the most guilty otherwise?"

Jenny looked at her. "That's not what I'm doing. I'm not just picking who looks guilty. I'm trying to figure out what happened. Helen had the code and gave it to Lizzy. Sally we know had the code but which of them hated Mickey more? Mickey messed with the dynamics of Sally's company and possibly its success or failure, but Lizzy seems more personally hurt by Mickey. They both had the code. They were both there the night Mickey died. And neither has an alibi that we know of."

Cherry turned a couple other blocks over and shrugged. "I guess you need to make a second door code block then."

Cherry picked up a block and labeled it like Jenny had. Then she pinned it next to Sally's block and moved Jenny's to sit by Lizzy Rose.

"Okay," Jenny said, looking at the board. "I guess that works."

Cherry smirked. "I just came to let you know the others went to dinner and it's time to join them. But, you know, I'm happy to help however I can."

"Dinner?" Jenny asked. "Is it that late?" She should have known.

"It's late." Cherry plucked several threads from Jenny's sleeve. "But it's not bad. Are you hungry?"

"Not really," Jenny admitted, but it was time to come out and rejoin the others. The murder board loomed behind them, and Jenny bit her lip. "We can go if you want."

Cherry looked up. "Really?"

"Of course." Jenny stacked up her extra quilt squares so they wouldn't be in anyone's way.

Cherry grabbed the door handle and paused. "Would you mind if we left through the convention? I wanted to sneak a peek at the booths. They open tomorrow, right?"

"Tomorrow afternoon," Jenny confirmed. In the hall the sounds of construction had gotten louder. Jenny hadn't noticed them before. And now the voices and bustle of construction held its own kind of mystery. "That's a great idea. I'd love to see the progress they're making."

The two of them made their way down the hall and turned down the grand staircase. "Oh my," Cherry said in hushed exclamation. "It's a little fabric city. How did they do all this?"

Jenny had no response. More of the designers and manufacturers had begun putting booths together than Jenny had seen the day before. Booths were popping up in everything from bright florals to deep reproduction civil war prints. The vibrancy of the whole room had escalated.

As they walked onto the floor, Cherry couldn't seem to hold still. "I can't believe we get to see all this happening."

Jenny followed her around, watching as designers and construction teams worked together.

"By tomorrow morning it's going to be amazing," Jenny admitted. The touch of awe that settled in her chest felt raw and open. "I'm a little jealous of these guys, you know. I always thought I'd like to try designing."

"Why didn't you?" Cherry asked. As they reached the bottom of the steps, they saw a woman pull out a drill and started connecting several sheets of hard plastic panels in what might be a geodesic snow globe.

"I don't know . . . I never pushed the plan. You know how it is."

Cherry looked at her, lips pursed. "Well, then do it. No one is stopping you from being your best self but you. Get out there and try, Mrs. Jenny Doan."

"Oh my goodness." Jenny's face warmed. For a moment, she allowed herself to imagine that she'd managed to design a fabric line that she and everyone else loved. Today, instead of walking around searching for a murderer, she would be setting up a booth with her own work that would seed someone else's inspiration. "Come on, I want to show you something."

Jenny led the way into the modern regency display at the Harper Wovens booth. No one was there, and Cherry did a slow circle, taking in her first good look at a booth in process.

"Did they make that?" Cherry looked at the huge floral chandelier dangling overhead. She stood underneath it, taking in the size and style of the gorgeous light fixture.

"I'm pretty sure. Isn't it beautiful?" Jenny admired the massive effort it must have taken to create such a large piece.

Across the booth a lilac fabric panel swung open, and Hugo Hensen strode in. He stopped when he saw them, his bright blue suit making it impossible not to notice him. "Jenny."

"Hugo," she replied. "You must be busy with the booths opening tomorrow. How's yours going?"

"It's already done. My team started working on it this morning." He ran a hand over his pale hair, glistening with product, and stood there as if waiting for her to say something.

"That's great . . . you haven't seen Sally, have you? I love the way her booth looks."

"Yeah, I guess it's all right. Well, Sally's not here." Hugo passed the women and paused at a table with a giant blooming flower bulb. The plant had red lilies the size of small dinner plates.

Hugo turned his fan friendly smile on Cherry. "Hello, I'm Hugo. It's so nice to meet you."

"You too." Cherry only glanced at him. "What is that flower? It's gorgeous." She circled past him and picked up the plant. "I need to find more of these."

Hugo's face fell so quickly it was almost comical. "Now I'm being passed up for the flora and fauna." When she stared at him, he softened. "Sorry. It's been a long day. I don't know where Sally is." He dropped onto the little couch. "I was going to wait here. You're welcome to join me."

"No, no. It's fine." Jenny watched Cherry turn the plant, admiring the bloom. "Have you checked the tag, Cherry? We should probably get going."

She pulled a red tag from the plant and opened it, then put it back. "That's a card." Cherry set the pot down. "I'll ask Sally later."

"A card?" Jenny looked closer and realized the card was the same red as the notecards delivered to Mickey earlier.

Hugo looked at the card and rolled his eyes. "It's probably for Owen. Like I said Sally, got it for someone special. Those two make me crazy."

"They're not together though, are they?" Jenny hadn't ever seen their relationship like that.

Footsteps startled Jenny, and she turned to see Sally coming into the booth behind them.

"Sally." Hugo stood to greet her with a kiss on the cheek. "I wanted to let you know that I'll be busy during the Q&A tonight. I'm so sorry. I was hoping Lizzy could take over for me. Will that work?"

Sally's brow furrowed. "Oh, but you know people are going to be disappointed if you're not there."

"I'm just a small label. That's why I like hanging out with you. And I'm your favorite, right?" It was a flippant question, but he held her eye until she shoved him away.

"You know I'll take care of it. Thanks for letting me know."

Sally got another side kiss from Hugo, and he

swept out of the booth without a backward glance.

Sally watched him go, removing her coat and a turquoise scarf. Its tiny yellow polka dots were a happy brightness to her solemn persona as she offered her hand to Jenny. "It looks like I'm in the business of doing favors, so, what can I do for you?"

She had regained her sense of calm. Jenny shook her head. "Nothing. We were just looking around before dinner." She waved at Cherry, who was still running a finger over the stout leaves of the bulb and cooing softly to it. "Though I think Cherry might be enjoying your plants more than the fabric."

She laughed, but Sally made a face. "Oh, who brought that? Do you want it? I'm allergic to flowers. The pollen is terrible."

"I'd love to have it. Are you sure?" Cherry picked up the plant, holding it securely in both arms. "I can take it upstairs now if that's alright."

Sally gave a disinterested shrug, and Cherry was already carrying her newly acquired Christmas plant up the stairs.

Sally went to one of the tables at the back of the booth and pulled a stack of pamphlets out to organize.

"Would you like some help?" Jenny picked up a similar stack of pamphlets and sorted them the way Sally was. "I wasn't sure if you'd be here."

Sally pursed her lips. "I shouldn't be. Owen and I left after we found out about Mickey. I only came back because I knew there was too much to do. And sitting in an empty apartment sounded like a great way for me to claw my eyes out."

"How much did you know about Mickey's design process?" Jenny prodded Sally carefully.

"I don't usually get in my designers' business too much, so I don't know much. Lizzy didn't enjoy working with her. She did a lot of second guessing herself." Sally took a full stack of pamphlets to another table and positioned them on a clear stand. "One time Mickey painted this entire piece of super bright geometric patterns, and when Lizzy started several coordinating prints, Mickey announced that they were terrible and destroyed them."

"Well that sounds . . . rocky." Jenny took another stack of pamphlets.

"That's being polite."

Sally moved to the back of the booth where several extra boxes and cases were stored. As Sally got into the top box, Jenny rallied her courage.

"Did she ever tell you how long it took her to make the line she submitted?"

Sally pulled out an extra roll of fabric clips while she considered Jenny's question. She shook her head and moved back to the booth.

A Body in Redwork

"I don't think so. She talked about working on it for a long time. But she couldn't get it worked out until last summer."

Jenny nodded. "Lizzy hasn't said anything about what she and Helen saw in this year's fabric book?"

Sally was in the middle of clipping two sections of the fabric panel walls together but stopped to look at Jenny.

"I haven't seen Lizzy all day. What's wrong with the book?" She let the fabric go and turned to face Jenny. "Did I mess something up?"

"Not you. Mickey." Jenny tugged at a string in her pocket and wrapped it around her finger. "Mickey's line was stolen." Sally stared at her, then turned and fished through piles of papers in a box before pulling out a fabric menu like the ones they'd been displaying only moments before. "What do you mean? Her line is fine. This is her line."

She spread the pamphlet out, showing a full page of the new Harper Wovens Organic Cottons by Mickey Stevens. The line was beautiful in rich jewel tones. Swirls of color danced around florals and teacups and tiny little animals. The teacups were detailed down to the blue and white scenes that echoed the real china Jenny's grandmother had owned. Jenny lifted the page, searching the delicate design of the teacups. Sure enough, Jenny saw the evidence right there.

She set the page back down on the table and pointed to a pink teacup. "This is the proof." The design across the teacup was capped with a straight line, and right above it was a tiny version of the name Helen. "Helen Derrick signed her fabric here. Mickey took her friend's artwork and sold it as her own."

"Oh my gosh." Sally was breathing quickly, and Jenny walked her to the little couch, shoving Sally's coat and polka dotted scarf to the ground.

"I'm sorry." Jenny perched herself on the foot of the settee. "I have several friends mixed up in this . . . one of them is you. I just found out that Mickey stole the line today, and I don't know what the right thing to say is, but I didn't want to hide this from you. You need to know."

Sally's face shifted, her brow furrowing. "And Lizzy knew?"

Jenny nodded. "I don't know when she realized, but she and Helen fought with Mickey about it the night she died."

"Oh wow. That's probably what she was trying to talk to me about." Sally's face was in her hand, her breathing still shaky and shallow. "What do we do now? If we print this, we could get sued. What do I do? I've put so much into this."

"Have you considered asking Helen Derrick to take her place? I don't know if she has the same social media following, but it would probably be the easiest thing to do."

"I don't think I've ever met Helen." Sally still looked like she wanted to cry, but Jenny's suggestion pulled her out of her spiral. "You said she's here? Can you introduce me?"

Jenny pictured Helen all waxy pale and worried like she'd looked that morning, but introducing the two would be a great first step to fixing things. "I'll check with her to make sure, but I think so."

Sally nodded and held onto her fabric pamphlet like it could save her life, when in reality it was tearing them apart.

7

Jenny moved quickly down the hall, pausing briefly at the door to the storage room. She could almost see the edge of her design board. She wanted to go look at it again, but Cherry was waiting for her. She was glad Sally hadn't known about Mickey's lie. But how did her apparent innocence fit into the scheme of information Jenny had found?

Reluctantly, she continued down the hall to the corner room. Cherry stood at the big corner window. The sewing machines were at a standstill, and the single red flower was in the windowsill. She had popped her hip to the side and was staring at the little plant, pinching her bottom lip in thought. The red card was no longer there.

Jenny pushed the door open, intentionally creating enough noise to be noticed. Cherry started and glanced over her shoulder briefly.

"Are you ready?" she asked, taking several steps backward while keeping an eye on the red blooms.

"I think so," Jenny answered from the doorway. "It's nice. The plant, I mean."

"Yeah." Cherry hesitated, leaning her head to the side and watching it. "I think it's going to be good."

The plant sat dutifully on the windowsill with no card in sight. Jenny looked closer, trying to see Cherry's vision. "Is it going to do tricks?"

Cherry laughed and turned. "No. It's not doing tricks, but it's going to help me decorate. Whoever sent it got it from the local florist. I just called up and ordered a dozen more. We're going to make this place so much better than Andi's plan." Cherry brushed a hand theatrically across her shoulder. "I win."

"The Christmas decorations? Are you still worried about that?" Jenny asked, amused by Cherry's competitive side. "I haven't even been thinking about them."

"That's why you have me. I already called Andi and told her not to bring any more decorations." Cherry grinned and bounced out of the room. "It's a good thing we caught Sally with that plant. I think I made Hugo nervous."

Jenny followed. "Not nervous . . . but I don't think

he was prepared for you to be more excited about the plant than meeting him."

"Can you blame me? That's an amaryllis. I know they're not that unusual this time of year, but I hadn't even considered it. Live florals are going to raise my game so much." Cherry scrunched her nose as she spoke and Jenny found herself laughing with her.

Cherry gathered her coat and gloves, stopping to look at the plant one more time. "I should thank Sally. Would you mind if we go out that way? I need to return her card anyway."

Cherry set the little red card on the side table while she pulled her coat on.

"You still have it." Jenny picked it up.

"Of course I have it. I wouldn't throw away someone else's note."

Jenny fished the card out of the envelope. As soon as she saw it, Jenny knew it was the same artist. Mickey was dead, and another card was being delivered. Her heart sank. The painting on the front was a beautiful stack of red, green, and white quilts tied up with a bow like a gift. The exquisite art was almost painful, knowing what was inside.

With more than a little hesitation, she peeled the card open.

Hillary Doan Sperry

What child is this who's laid to rest?
Your sister soon will be weeping.
No angels greet but demons meet.
A bloodline of falsehoods you're keeping.

This, this, is truth you'll sing,
your lies seek death on angel's wings.
Haste, haste, redeem fair chance,
you've taken from others by cheating.

The same chill clawed at Jenny's mind that she'd felt when she found the first poems. It wasn't over yet. Talking to Sally no longer felt like an optional thing. Jenny shoved the little card in the envelope. "Come on. We need to see Sally."

She was already down the hall before Helen's voice called out. "Cherry? Jenny! Are you guys still here?" Helen appeared at the top of the stairwell, relief spreading across her face. "Oh, thank goodness. Have either of you seen Lizzy Rose? I've been trying to call her for a while and she's not picking up."

Jenny hesitated, then beckoned to them both. "I haven't seen Lizzy but I need you to come downstairs. Sally Harper needs to meet you."

Jenny turned, her long legs carrying her down the hall quickly. Meeting Helen would be good closure for a piece of Mickey's deceit, but that wasn't why she was hurrying. Someone else at Harper Wovens was going to die if Jenny didn't find out who that card had been intended for.

Jenny flew down the stairs, hitting the bottom before Cherry or Helen had reached the top. She took a breath as she reached the back of the Harper Wovens booth and slipped between the fabric panels. Nothing had changed except that Sally wasn't there anymore.

She stepped out into the aisle. In the chaos of workers and designers now hitting the mad rush phase of set up, the only person she recognized was Owen Teak.

"Owen?" She walked up behind him, but he didn't seem to notice. He was talking to a woman in the neighboring booth. She had dark hair and bright lipstick and was currently sewing fabric vines to the poles of her company's booth. A large sign advertising their company as Pears & Gin Fabric Design hung from the upper pole of the booth.

Jenny tapped him on the shoulder. "Owen? I'm looking for Sally. I need to talk to you both."

Owen half turned, looking puzzled by her question. "What do you need me for?"

The note burned in her hand, and she looked at the young lady and tried to be discreet. "I'm worried about the situation with Mickey. I think it's happening again."

It probably wasn't vague enough, but it had only been a couple of days. Maybe the other designers hadn't gossiped too badly and didn't know Mickey had died.

The girl's face went white, and Jenny knew she was wrong.

"Did someone else get hurt or. . . ?" She didn't finish and Jenny didn't say anything as she gripped Owen's sleeve.

He excused himself and followed Jenny back to his own booth. "You shouldn't have said that. Maggie gets nervous."

"It's important."

Owen nodded. "Do we need to call the police back?"

"I think so." Jenny held up the red card. "It's happening again. Did you notice the flower pot that was delivered here this afternoon?"

"Yeah. I think Sally bought it for Lizzy."

Jenny stopped. "But Sally's allergic."

"Yeah, but Lizzy isn't."

"And she gave the flower to my assistant. Why would she do that if it was for Lizzy?"

Owen made a face and stepped around Jenny. "Nobody's been able to get in touch with Lizzy. She probably got embarrassed or something. Is this really why you think somebody's going to get killed?"

Jenny gave him the card, and his face blanched. He looked over his shoulder before he'd even read what was inside.

"Helen, wonderful to meet you! I've been wanting to talk to you." Sally's voice spilled through the fabric wall.

Jenny took the card back and grabbed Owen's hand, pulling him toward the conversation they were missing. "Come on, we should be talking about this with her."

On the other side of the fabric, Cherry and Helen stood shaking hands with Sally. Helen looked shell-shocked, and Sally looked like a vulture.

"Jenny told me about what happened," Sally said, Helen's hand clasped between both of her own. "I can't believe we didn't know Mickey's fabric was your artwork."

"Is this Helen?" Owen stepped into the conversation and snatched Helen's hand away from Sally. "I want to apologize for taking this as far as we did without your permission."

"It's not your fault." Helen pulled her hand back and wrapped her arms around her waist.

Sally stepped closer, tightening the tiny circle. "Mickey talked so much about her work and how she had put her heart into those paintings. We just believed her."

"It's a terrible thing." Owen's voice dripped with heartache, and Jenny couldn't help thinking about his conversation with the designer at the neighboring booth. He hadn't seemed heartbroken then.

Helen looked ready to sink into herself, so Jenny stepped forward and wrapped an arm around her. "Sally, what was it you liked about Helen's artwork?"

Sally nodded mechanically. "Of course, yes, umm, it's beautiful. It's inventive and fresh and I want to have the artist on my team."

Helen tensed and bit her lip. "Thank you. But I just can't see myself promoting this line. It would be too painful. I know she sold it to you. That's done. But I can't see myself standing up and saying I'm Mickey or that it's mine when everyone believes it's hers. I won't. I'm sorry."

"No, it wouldn't be like that." Owen raised his hands. "Maybe we could. . .well, if we tell people about who you are. That you knew Mickey. . ."

Helen shook her head, her eyes not leaving the ground. "I'm just not comfortable with any scenario I can see right now."

"What if I do it?" Jenny cut in. She wasn't sure

why she said it except that Helen was so distraught and Sally was trying so hard to make something work. "I could promote the line. Sally, you could pay Helen off the proceeds and I would do a couple promo things. Then we're done, and hopefully both of you can come out of this in a better position."

Helen released a huge breath. "And I don't have to say it's mine?"

"No. Absolutely not." Sally's eyes were wide as she looked between Jenny and Helen. "We really only need someone this week for all the promo shots and events."

Jenny tensed as she realized she would have to be onstage with them throughout the week. She wasn't sure she should do that.

"Cherry?" Jenny shot a questioning look at her assistant, who raised her eyebrows and shrugged.

"I'll see what we can do," Cherry said, raising her eyebrows.

"Great." Owen clapped his hands as if it was decided. "We can talk about the rest later."

Helen tensed. "The rest?"

"No. Just for the week." Jenny wasn't about to commit to a long-term deal without checking that it was really feasible. She still had another job to do.

Sally pushed Owen back. "Only till Saturday. Not even the whole week."

"Three days." Jenny looked at Helen. "I'll do it if Helen's okay with it."

Sally and Owen froze, watching the scared young woman.

Finally Helen held her hand out. "If Jenny will mediate this, I'm fine with it."

Color washed through Sally's face and Owen dropped his hands, puffing his chest out in a huge breath.

"This is going to be a good thing," he said. "I can send you details about what we need."

The two of them turned to leave and Jenny reached out grabbing Owen's arm. "Wait! I have to show you this."

Jenny stopped them but Helen spoke up. "I have to go. I'm sorry. I need some air."

"I'll go with you," Cherry said. "Call me if you need me."

Jenny glanced back as Cherry escorted Helen through the booths but quickly turned back to the pair of shop owners. "A note was delivered to Harper Wovens earlier today with the flower you gave to Cherry. How many of your designers at Harper Wovens have a sister?"

Jenny didn't have to open the card to hear the opening lines of the poem. *What child is this who's laid to rest? Your sister soon will be weeping.*

Sally looked startled. "Well, I'm not sure, we don't ask their family relations when we hire them. Lizzy—" Sally stopped herself and looked at Owen as if she'd just made a mistake. "Uh, I mean, yeah. Uh, Lizzy has a sister." There was a tremor in her voice. She swung her gaze back to Owen.

"And I have all brothers." Owen stepped in, his smile masking any other emotion. "Do they count?"

Jenny gave a polite laugh and turned to Sally. "Does Lizzy get along with her family?"

Sally shook her head, tying her scarf into a loose knot. "I mean, all families have some issues, right?" Her voice rose in pitch. "What makes you ask that?"

Jenny held the card out to Owen and Sally so they could read it. Sally sucked in a breath while Owen just stared.

Sally turned. "I have to go."

"I can get that to the police." Owen said, trying to take the card.

Jenny didn't let go. "Hold on." She snapped a picture of the verse and gave it to Owen.

He was looking after Sally but turned back to point at Jenny. "Can you be at the Q&A tonight?"

Jenny nodded, and Owen flashed a smile before he ran after Sally.

"Well, that was weird." Jenny pulled her phone out and typed "Lizzy Rose fabric designer" into her phone. Up popped a string of websites dedicated to the fabric designer, with a few random sites for unrelated people. Jenny clicked through social media sites and blogs that were not nearly as interesting as they would have been another time.

There was nothing about her family on any of them.

Jenny clicked on another site and didn't see anything except someone posting about a friendiversary. Jenny scrolled a little farther and saw pictures of the dark-haired Lizzy in various places, with all manner of snacks and friends to show how much fun she was having.

Jenny clicked away from the page and this time typed in "Harper Wovens family-ties" The search pulled up old television shows and a facebook profile for Sally Harper. None of the posts seemed related. She clicked on the profile and stopped. At the top of the screen was the same friendiversary post she'd seen on Lizzy Rose's page.

The post wasn't for each other but showed an older man and a young man dancing across the screen. Both were Harpers.

"It's not so unusual that a person could be trying to be friendly to their boss's family," Jenny muttered. Jenny scrolled through a couple more posts and came back to that one. "But it's a little

strange that both Lizzy and Sally were tagged."
Jenny tapped the screen. "What if Sally and Lizzy
are related?"

The two women looked nothing like each other.
Sally was tall and blonde with a long oval face,
while Lizzy was shorter with dark hair and freckles
over the bridge of her nose.

Cherry looked at the post and then scrolled
through more carefully. Sally didn't have much
family listed in her relationships. As Jenny clicked
through them she made it to a brother's page and in
his family relations, both Sally and Lizzy Rose were
listed as sisters.

"A bloodline of falsehoods. Talk about the family
secrets?"

Jenny didn't understand. She flipped over to her
pictures and scanned the poems. All three poems
had harped on lying or telling the truth. It was
almost like he gave them a warning to see if they
would come clean. The most recent one told them
to sing the truth or seek death. Mickey's had
mentioned a fabric of lies. Jenny flipped through the
images and saw again the first note. *Tell truth or
lose what you most treasure.*

Life is definitely most treasured . . . but whose
was the next target?

Jenny moved into the Harper Wovens booth and

looked around. It had come together nicely. She picked up a few random stacks of paper that had been left behind in the rush of the two owners to leave.

They'd definitely been nervous. Jenny moved around the back of the booth and set the extra pamphlet stacks down. Jenny scanned the boxes that had been tucked away there. One had several folders inside. She was still alone behind the booth, so she flipped the folder open. Inside was a stack of overdue bills, but in front of them Jenny picked up a printout of orders.

It looked like pre-orders for Mickey's Organic Cottons line. There were a lot of them; at the bottom of the page they totaled over fifty thousand dollars.

Jenny's jaw dropped. "And all since Mickey died."

Jenny replaced the papers and did a quick look around. She couldn't help the theory forming in her head. At least one of the Harper Wovens owners was lying and if lies were what bothered the killer, Jenny had just narrowed the potential targets down to one of two people.

Of course Owen had never been a designer. She thought about the way he'd looked when Jenny had shown him the note. He had barely reacted when she'd let them read it. And when he'd seen it the first time it was almost like he recognized it.

Was Owen upset that Sally and Lizzy were lying about their relationship? Killing Mickey certainly seemed to do wonders for her fabric sales. Did he think having their relationship known would help sales?

A crash sounded and Jenny jumped. She hurried past the fabric wall and into the Harper Wovens booth. Maggie was bent over, picking up a heavy pole that appeared to have fallen from the Pears & Gin booth.

"Are you alright?" Jenny moved to help her lift it.

"Yes. I just pushed the wrong pin. These things are sturdy, but you'd be amazed how little the connectors are that keep them upright."

Jenny helped her move it to the side and Maggie thanked her. And an alert chimed on her phone. It was Owen.

> *- Don't forget. Meet Sally at the park in five.*

A creak sounded, and footsteps pounded away. Behind Jenny, a pole crashed to the ground. A glint of movement and light caught Jenny's eye before someone screamed. The huge chandelier overhead jerked out of place. Jenny cried out and jumped away as poles and fabric came down around her.

8

Screams punctured the air like a sewing machine needle, engulfing Jenny's mind until the sound of crashing metal stopped. For six seconds nothing existed except the fear of what might happen. Then someone called her name. The chandelier hung precariously overhead and across the mess, a woman with tall blonde hair picked her way through the half collapsed booth.

The woman was a good foot shorter than Jenny, but she made up for it with a pale pouf of shimmering blonde hair piled high above her head and tied up in the back with a handmade bow that matched her the booth behind her.

"Stay still," the woman said, her southern accent even stronger than Cherry's. "Are you alright?"

Jenny slowly looked up. Only a handful of poles had come down on the side of the booth adjacent to Pears & Gin, but somehow the cross poles had caught against each other and the chandelier was lodged just over the couch. It hovered over Jenny, not touching her at all.

"I think so. Just shaken up." Jenny wasn't sure if she said the words out loud or not but she blinked and turned to the stranger. "Did you see anyone running away?"

"No. The poles started falling and I couldn't keep my booth upright anymore. Darlin', I'm just glad to see you're all right. My name is Ruby Carter. I'm the owner of Pears & Gin."

Pears & Gin. The name rang a bell and Jenny looked up. "Maggie works for you."

It was more of a realization than a question. Ruby laughed. "She sure does. Maggie Sun. She's a genius. If you haven't seen her fabric yet, you will." Ruby looked around. "I'm not seeing her right now, but she's around. Now, I don't know if it was my booth or Harpers that had the problem, but all I saw was my palm tree collapsing, and I knew something had gone wrong. This whole booth is solid. I don't know how it happened."

"It's strange, isn't it?" Jenny tried to remember what she'd seen before the accident, but it hurt her head. There had been footsteps and a glint of light—that was probably just the poles. Except, the poles all seemed to be wrapped in fabric.

120

A Body in Redwork

The shorter woman looked Jenny over. When she was satisfied with her general health, she patted Jenny's shoulder, causing her to wince at an injury she didn't know she had. Ruby then waved to the crowd. "I'll gather up some of these guys and we'll help put the framework of the Harper Wovens booth back up. I'm just glad you weren't hurt."

Jenny nodded. The little flash she'd seen repeated in her mind. Metal clanged to the ground as one of the helpers grabbed a pole and Jenny jumped, heart still thumping rapidly in her chest..

Slowly, she made her way to the door. Someone called to a bystander to lift some of the framework. It sounded like Owen's voice had finally joined them, but Jenny didn't look back.

Jenny took a deep breath as the front door opened and cold, fresh air hit her face. Cherry stood at the railing with her phone to her ear. "That's impossible. You need to fix that. I need those plants."

Jenny slumped against the railing. Something must have bumped her on the way down because her shoulder ached.

"You will not believe what just happened," Cherry announced, holding her phone to her chest to block the sound. "'Someone,'" she put the word in air quotes, "canceled my order of Amaryllis plants. She called back to explain that I might still see a charge on my card until the refund goes through. Can you believe Andi would do that?"

"The Harper Wovens booth just collapsed on me," Jenny said softly.

Cherry didn't say anything for a second and then leaned back on the railing. "Okay, you win. Are you all right?"

Jenny smiled at her. "I'm fine. I don't know what happened. I was helping Maggie move a pole, and then she was gone and the booth had collapsed. Amazingly I wasn't hurt, but my nerves are fried."

Cherry shook her head. "I'm calling Ron."

"That would be really good. And I'm going to go sit down." Jenny pointed herself toward one of the benches in front of the bakery and together she and Cherry made their way across the street.

"I wish I'd brought my car." Cherry reached up, putting her own scarf around Jenny's neck and scanned the street.

"No, it's fine. I'm fine. The cold air is honestly good. I feel clearer now than I did inside." Jenny rubbed her hands together and pulled her phone out. She pushed at the screen and got no response. Cherry took the phone from her, and Jenny relaxed.

"You just had a booth fall on you. Not by any fault of your own. You don't need to deal with any of this. That's someone else's job." Cherry dialed, and Jenny heard Ron pick up. She released a breath, reveling in the calming effect his voice had on her.

When Cherry hung up, Jenny took her phone back and frowned. "I didn't get to talk to him."

Cherry shook a finger at her and hooked an arm through her elbow. "You don't need to do anything more complicated than walking right now. We're going over here to wait for Ron."

Cherry's phone rang, and they stopped in front of the patio for her to answer it. Jenny swayed slightly and shook her head, grateful she could shake her head without aching now.

Across the street, a crew was setting up chairs in front of a temporary outdoor stage in Penney park for the designers Q&A. The work had drawn a crowd, including her son, Jake, and daughter-in-law, Misty, filming a video to share the fun of the event with Missouri Star Quilt Company fans who couldn't be in Hamilton this week. They had set up large heaters surrounding the audience area and behind the stage. The stage spanned the width of the small park, with a large awning extending into the audience.

In front of the stage, Misty wore a full winter coat and a beanie topped with a furry puff, plus a beaming smile. Jake stood filming her near a small gathering of tourists. Jake panned up to the "magic tree," and Misty said something that made the crowd laugh. The "magic tree" was a large tree set right on the edge of Main Street. Every year it was wrapped in rainbow-colored Christmas lights, and every night when it lit up, the street around it glowed.

Jenny couldn't help watching. The lights weren't on yet, but the tree wasn't what had her attention. It was an odd day when Jenny walked through town and didn't run into someone from her family. She loved it most when she caught them in action, working together like Jake and Misty were now.

She looked back to see that Cherry was still busy.

"I'm going over there." Jenny whispered to Cherry, who had a credit card gripped between her teeth.

"No problem," Cherry muttered and pulled the card from her mouth. "I've got this."

Jenny checked the street before crossing. The crowd had grown in the few minutes she'd waited and Misty and Jake had been swallowed by them. Circling the group slowly Jenny saw Sally watching the street, her hand to her neck and her fingers working her collar nervously. With half a desire to keep an eye on Sally and halfway wanting to finally

see what it was like to live the life of a designer,
Jenny moved toward her. She rolled her shoulders
as she went and Jenny's phone dinged.

> *- I'm on my way*

It was Ron. Jenny texted back.

> *- It's okay. I'm going to stay for a bit. I'm
> helping Harpers.*

As Jenny worked on the message, the lights of
Hamilton's "magic tree" turned on, lighting the
crowd in the dimming sky. It wasn't fully dark yet,
but everyone's attention went to the tree.

Her phone rang and Jenny picked up. "Are you
sure you're okay? Cherry said there was some kind
of accident."

"There was," Jenny agreed, stepping around a
cluster of quilters. "I just needed to take care of
something. I'm really fine."

"What happened?" The concern in Ron's voice
made Jenny stop. She couldn't keep brushing him
off.

"I really don't know. I think it was an accident."

"You think?" His tone intensified and Jenny
moved away from the group.

"Yes. I think it was an accident. No one was

around except one little girl who ran off when the poles fell." There wasn't really a good way to tell your spouse a metal booth had collapsed on you, so Jenny pushed forward. "Nothing hit me though. It all got stuck around a chandelier and I was fine."

Ron hesitated and Jenny could almost feel him coming to terms with her crazy experiences again. "Let me know when you're ready to come home, okay?"

Jenny played with a tiny spool of thread she'd found in her pocket. "Can you come get me at the park in a little bit? I'm helping with the Q&A tonight."

"Are you sure everything's all right?" Ron sounded worried, and Jenny walked toward the backstage area.

"Everything's fine."

Ron was quiet. She tried not to think about how well he could read her.

"I mean, as fine as it can be right now."

When he finally spoke, she wasn't prepared for his question. "This is hard for you, isn't it?"

In the short time since Mickey had passed, Jenny hadn't taken much time at all to see if and how she was dealing with Mickey's loss.

Jenny looked around. The park was filling up with guests as the night got closer to dusk. The heaters made a rosy glow, and overhead strings of lights were hung all around the venue with floodlights filling in the stage area. People pushed closer as she circled the crowd, but no one seemed to be listening to her conversation. She moved toward the back of the stage anyway.

"I still can't believe she's gone. All I can remember is the playful, happy Mickey. The one that brought presents for everyone because she couldn't stand for anyone to feel left out. And now, the rest of my friends are considered murder suspects." She hissed the last part into the phone, hoping her lips had found the speaker and it would pick up her low tones. She didn't want to say it again, and she didn't want anyone else to hear it.

"I'm sorry, Jenny. Is Helen still at the top of their list?" Ron's voice was sympathetic, and she wished for a moment that she was sitting at home with him like Cherry told him she would be.

As the announcer got on stage and welcomed everyone to the Designers Q&A with his big, booming voice, Jenny knew it was too late to be anywhere else. After getting buried in Harper Wovens' convention booth, Jenny had moved Sally well above Helen and Liz on the suspect list.

"I don't know. Probably at the top of the police's list. I think most of the other girls have been cleared.

There's just no motive for them. And it wasn't Helen, so I don't know what the police have found, but I'm trying to make sure she's not the only one on their list." Jenny moved into the backstage area. It wasn't hidden by any means, but the designers had lined up. Sally stood at the far end, beckoning to her.

Ron hesitated. "You have a list of suspects? But that's not your job."

"It's never my job." Jenny thought of the other times she'd been in this kind of situation.

"But you always end up in the middle of it." Ron didn't sound like he got the joke. His anxious tone needled her gut. "Just be careful. Give the police a chance to figure this out. Whoever it is, let them do their job."

"I'll be careful. I've got too many commitments here." Jenny tripped on a quilt someone had stashed under the stage as she passed the other designer guests, but caught herself quickly. "I better go. I love you."

"I love you too. I'll see you in an hour."

Jenny hung up. The stage stood a good four feet off the ground. From her vantage point the large wooden platform would easily hold the designers that were assembled at the back. The announcer was still accounting for the different companies who would be sharing their "innermost design secrets" with the crowd. Jenny looked out at everyone, in awe of the fact that most of the world had no idea that Mickey had died or that another designer could be gone soon.

Sally waved her over and Jenny bypassed the rest of the designers to catch her at the end of the line.

Sally gave a shaky smile, shooting another glance at the street. "Have you seen Lizzy? I don't know why she isn't here."

"Does she know she's supposed to be here?" Jenny scanned the crowd too, but she wasn't looking for Lizzy. Owen's tall figure was stationed at the far end of the crowd. She had missed him on her way around but his eyes were glued to the pair of them.

"I told her the schedule last night, but she's been all over the place. I haven't seen her all day." Sally had twisted the corner of her collar into a rope and as it popped out of her grip and unwound she flattened it against her shirt and started over.

"I'm sure she'll be here. She would at least tell you if she couldn't come, right?"

Sally nodded, her eyes on the street and the people as they moved forward again.

"Sally, where were you Monday night?"

Sally pulled her gaze back, apparently surprised by the question. "I had dinner with Lizzy and Owen."

Jenny shook her head, "What about after that? Late, like into Tuesday morning?"

"I was sleeping." She gave Jenny a funny look then and Jenny looked away. You couldn't corroborate sleeping very well unless she could talk to the neighbors. "I think your rental is down the street from where we were staying before. Is that right?"

"Why are you asking? Because it sounds like you think I might be guilty of something."

"No, that's not it. I just wanted to clear it up. I've been looking into things a little bit. I just have too many friends involved in these murders to sit back and not care." Jenny jerked to the audience when they all started to cheer and the line finally started to move.

Designers went onstage to introduce themselves and sit at a panel where the audience would get to question them along with pre-chosen questions to start a discussion. It's just a show. Jenny had always loved theater. She knew how to put on a show.

"I can understand that," Sally said, walking with her. "But I was really just home. I can give you the address if you want to check it out."

130

A Body in Redwork

Jenny wrote the address into her phone and the group stopped as the first round of designers took their seats.

"What about Owen?" Jenny could almost feel him watching them. She tried not to look too anxious as she waited for Sally's response. "Was he home all night?"

Sally's eyes blinked up at her in surprise. "Jenny? We don't have that kind of relationship."

Jenny's eyes widened and she shook her head. "I didn't mean that. I just wondered if you'd heard him leave or anything."

Sally's mouth formed an 'O' and Jenny's cheeks warmed to a hellish temperature.

"No. I didn't hear anything," Sally finally said. Jenny nodded.

The information wasn't even reliable. Jenny hurriedly turned away and followed the designer in front of her toward the stairs. Jenny's feet found the same dislodged quilt that she'd tripped on the first time she'd passed this point and she gave a quick look to see if it needed to be put away.

The heavy green quilt looked familiar. A star made with green and blue prints staggered with solid colored blocks like a glamorous nine patch. Jenny grabbed the quilt to move it and dropped it almost immediately.

"Something's in there," Jenny said.

She shoved the corner of the quilt back under the edge of the stage and stepped away. Suddenly the familiarity of the quilt clicked into place. It was the same pattern as the quilt Mickey had been wrapped in, just different fabrics. The corner lay folded over the rest of the quilt exposing a tiny stitched flower in the corner. It was the only stitching on the quilt. Something about that tickled the edge of her consciousness.

"Oh no." Jenny's hand went to her mouth. "Everybody needs to back up."

She pushed people away. Both Vana Suze and Hugo Hensen stood at the stage, not noticing anyone until Jenny shoved them to the side.

Cries of annoyance and frustration sounded around her. It was several seconds before she realized the announcer was leaning over the back of the stage, looking down at her.

"What's going on?" he asked, genuine concern in his voice.

Jenny hadn't moved the quilt yet. If she found what she thought she would, it would become real. Mickey's body had been found the night before last. It hadn't even been two days. Jenny pulled back the quilt and gasped, a sudden breath that stuck in her throat.

A Body in Redwork

A life size doll lay painted under the stage, her hair in pigtails and lips green with huge blue circles painted on her cheeks.

Jenny looked up at the announcer. "We need the police. Lizzy Rose is dead."

9

"You saw she was wearing her designer's pin, right?" Jenny leaned toward Officer Dunn, trying to see if he'd written what she'd said.

"Excuse me." Dunn pulled his tablet back, his eyebrow raised in suspicion. Sadly, suspicion was better than the bored expression he'd had for the rest of their conversation.

Across the park, Officer Wilkins was talking with Sally, who'd been sobbing since they'd found Lizzy's body.

"And is there anything else you'd like us to know about Lizzy or the situation? Because I really hate it when you come chasing us down later. So feel free to share all your unfounded suspicions now." Officer Dunn rolled his eyes and waved for Jenny to speak.

"Did Owen Teak give you the notecard that was

sent to Harpers before Lizzy died?"

"It was sent before? When?"

"This afternoon . . . I'm not really sure exactly when." She looked over her shoulder to where the body had been surrounded by officers. "It was sent in a flowering plant."

Dunn nodded and made a note."Do you know where it is?"

"Yes. But I don't think it will help you. It's just a plant and it's been handled by a lot of people."

"We'd still like to see it if it's available." Jenny nodded and looked back at Sally. She was shaking her head as Officer Wilkins led her toward the police car waiting at the side of the road.

"What are they doing?" The panic in Jenny's voice surprised her, but she couldn't seem to stop it. "They can't think Sally did this."

"Why not?" Officer Dunn asked. "Do you know where Sally was over the last three to four hours?"

"Yes." Jenny had been with Sally several times over the last couple of hours, but not consistently. "I mean, around six-thirty I spoke with her for about twenty minutes. And then I saw her again maybe five minutes later for another fifteen to twenty minutes."

Dunn nodded and circled a pencil like he wanted her to keep going. "That accounts for her whereabouts between six-thirty and seven."

Jenny put her hands on her hips and glared at him.

"Okay, we'll be generous. Let's say seven-thirty." He looked at his watch. "It's nine, correct?" He waited for her to confirm the time. "Where were you around five?"

Jenny's teeth were clenched, and she had to force herself to loosen them. "I told you that. I was working on a sewing project. All of my friends saw me. In the same building where Sally was setting up her booth."

"And can any of you tell me that you saw or were with Sally during that time? Because I don't have anyone, so far, that can do that. Even her partner says he was somewhere else."

Jenny opened her mouth to speak and closed it. Owen was unaccounted for during that time too. "But Sally and Lizzy were sisters. Why would she kill her sister?"

The officer pulled his tablet out and made a note, but it probably included the caveat of "this came from an impassioned Jenny Doan" or "Jenny said this while trying to convince me she is smarter than us." Then he looked up at her, the bored expression back on his face. "I don't know why killers do what they do."

Jenny couldn't stand it. While Sally got shut into

a police car, she finished her statement. The crowd was finally dwindling, but not soon enough for people to avoid seeing Sally be driven away.

Meanwhile, the real killer was getting away with everything.

If only she knew who it was. The whole thing felt impossible.

Jenny pulled out her phone to make sure Ron was on his way and got tripped up by the image on the screen. It showed the inside of the card that had been left with Lizzy's body. They'd switched the lyrics from the more traditional "What Child is This" to its original form of "Greensleeves," and the haunting melody wound its hooks into Jenny's mind.

Alas my love you do me wrong
To lie and cheat to our faces,
I've held your secret, the truth I've known.
No longer to rest in my graces.

Greensleeves wasn't who she told,
Greensleeves was lying,
Greensleeves was of Harpers fold,
Now gone is my lady Greensleeves

It was the second verse of the Christmas carol

138

they had used to warn Lizzy . . . if she'd even received it. Just like they'd done to Mickey. Now that she knew who the plant had been intended for, Jenny couldn't help wondering where it had come from. Sally couldn't really be the one who had warned her sister about her impending death and then sobbed while the police accused her of murder.

The poem laid out the "lie" Lizzy had been guilty of. Being Sally's sister. Jenny could hardly believe that was why she'd been killed.

Owen Teak walked up as Jenny flipped the screen from the poem to the cover image on the card.

"How did you know it was Lizzy in there?" He sat next to her and leaned his elbows against his knees.

"I didn't." Jenny was only partly listening to him. The image of the front of the card showed a bed covered in a simple star quilt in green and white with a Christmas wreath on the end of the bed. Sitting on the bed was a dolly, her hair in pigtails with bright blue cheeks. Just like Lizzy had been painted. It was strange how closely the artist matched the girls to the dollies in the paintings. She couldn't decide if the girls were being painted to match existing cards or if the dolls were being added to the images.

"It's interesting that you discovered both the girls who died."

Jenny looked up from her phone screen. Owen was perched on the opposite end of the bench, watching her, hands braced against his knees and his tie loose around his neck.

"I didn't discover Mickey. Tilly did." Jenny gripped her phone and prayed Ron was on his way. "What are you saying Owen?"

Owen shook his head. "You've been worming your way into my company, and suddenly my people are dropping like flies."

"Lizzy and Mickey were both my friends. I would never do anything to hurt them."

"I hope not, because sometimes minding your own business is much safer than messing with someone else's."

Jenny's jaw sagged open. "Are you threatening me?"

"If you're not involved, then this doesn't seem like a very safe place to be and if you are . . . I can make sure you'll regret hurting my people."

Owen leaned forward, putting his face inches from hers. Jenny scrambled back on the bench and dropped her phone.

"Here." Owen leaned to get it before Jenny could. Instead of returning it, Owen gaped at the image on the screen. He flipped the screen to the next image and saw the poem. Jenny snatched her phone away, turning it off.

"Is that—it's another card isn't it?" Owen's face had gone white, his jaw tensed.

"Yeah. And now it's police evidence. Do you recognize something?" Jenny asked, watching Owen.

He swallowed and turned his lips down. "No. It's just bizarre. Wow."

"Bizarre?" After startling him like that she'd hoped for more than denial. "What did you know about Sally's and Lizzy's relationship? Did you know they were sisters like the poem says?"

Owen tipped his head and looked at her. "Did it say that? That's not how I understood it."

Jenny lifted her phone, the screen lighting back up. She flipped it from the cover image to the poem, then quoted the most telling parts. "She wasn't who she told . . . She was of Harpers fold? And if you remember the first one said your sister soon will be weeping. So yeah, sisters."

Owen flinched. "Mickey told you, didn't she?"

Jenny shrugged and looked away, pretending she knew what he referenced.

Owen growled under his breath, as headlights flashed across the park. "She never cared about anyone but herself." He scuffed at the ground and glared at Jenny. "I don't know how Mickey found out, but they weren't hurting anyone. Lizzy wanted it a secret. It wasn't Sally's choice. Lizzy didn't want people to think it was her sister's name that carried her."

"But Mickey found out while they were working together." Jenny let her logic tell the story, and Owen closed his eyes in defeat, confirming her suspicions.

"She held it over their heads daily. She used it to get anything she wanted. She wouldn't even use our pins. She wanted something special. As if being a Harper Wovens designer wasn't special enough."

Jenny put a hand out. "She didn't use your pins? But I saw hers."

"Mickey didn't want a pin. She wanted a charm. I didn't even know what that meant." Owen was getting angrier by the second. "You better not have anything to do with this. If you do, I swear." His fist clenched and unclenched as Jenny shifted away from him.

Officer Dunn called to him and Owen stood, unable to do anything while the police officer had his eye on him. Jenny walked toward the corner of the park by Main Street.

Wilkins stopped her as Ron pulled up. "Jenny, did

you give your statement yet? I know Dunn said he would talk with you."

"I did. I hope you got the information you need." Jenny started to pass him but turned back. "Just so you know. Owen Tcak, Sally's business partner, just threatened me. He seemed very protective of his business and designers. As if he'd do anything to keep them from being hurt."

Wilkins raised an eyebrow, and Jenny shrugged.

"Just thought you should know."

"Thank you. That's very good information. It fits the narrative we have going on right now." Wilkins made a note in his notebook.

Jenny bit her lip and looked back at Ron's car. The headlights had gone down, but it wouldn't be long before he came out after her. "Why did you take Sally in?"

"I don't have to tell you that and you know it."

"I do. Sally wouldn't kill her sister. Did you see how upset she was?"

"Maybe she was so upset because she'd lost her scarf."

Jenny pulled back. "Excuse me?"

"Sally told me that she'd lost her scarf. A black and white plaid one. And a deep orange-red one a couple days ago."

Jenny's stomach sank. "The murder weapon."

Officer Wilkins nodded. "The murder weapons, plural. I know you have lots of reasons to watch out for her, but forensic evidence doesn't lie. She used her own scarves to murder both those girls. She had opportunity, means, and motive."

"Lizzy wasn't strangled, though." Jenny narrowed her eyes at the officer.

His pencil froze. "How did you know that?"

"The markings on her neck were different than Mickey's. And it looked like blood in her hair. Just guessing, but if they used a scarf on Lizzy, she was probably already dead."

Wilkins shoved his notepad in his pocket. "Jenny. You have to stop that. You're not supposed to know those things."

Jenny shivered from more than the cold and tried to imagine where the scarf could have gone. "What was her motive to kill her sister?"

"Look, we only took her for questioning. She's not being locked up yet. And I don't think she meant to kill Lizzy. Lizzy was struck on the side of the head before she was strangled. Then she dressed her up as one of the designers to make her fit the profile. Get lumped in with whoever else she was going to kill. Even if it's an accident, it's still murder."

"That's accurate," Dunn said, walking up behind them. "But I don't know why he's telling you that."

A Body in Redwork

Wilkins grumbled something in agreement and turned to Jenny. "Thank you for your statement. We'll be in touch if we need anything else."

Jenny turned on her heel. Ron was waiting, and if the officers didn't want her help, she wasn't going to give it to them.

Jenny sat at home that evening with several variations of the lemoyne star laid out in front of her. She needed a distraction, and working on her sewing was the easiest way to relax. Thankfully the filming wasn't until later in the week since it was only the second time she'd looked at the pattern. She still had to decide how to put the block together in its simplest form.

Ron leaned his head out from the kitchen. "Are you ready for eclairs?"

Jenny looked up in surprise. "Didn't you just start working on those?"

"Oh no," Ron chuckled. "I started long before I knew you'd be needing a treat tonight." Eclairs were a family favorite, and Ron pulled out a plate with several of the sweet treats piled on it. "I was just putting the chocolate on top."

"Mmm." The sound escaped Jenny before she'd

acknowledged how right Ron was. His penchant for baking had more than once been exactly what she needed and, while it added to her waistline, it was a gift she wouldn't trade. "I'm surprised we don't have a passel of grandkids here begging to try one of these." Jenny lifted one of the delicate confections to her lips. Its thick chocolate coating covered vanilla cream and crispy pastry dough, ushering a wave of memories.

"Don't worry, I have enough to share."

Jenny let the flavors dance in her mouth before grinning back at him. "I don't doubt that one little bit."

"How is everyone doing? In town, I mean." Ron chose his own pastry and settled into the love seat next to Jenny. "After Mickey's death, I know there's got to be some trauma at Harpers, and losing Lizzy now, too."

Jenny nodded. "I found out tonight that Lizzy Rose was Sally Harpers sister."

Ron's eclair paused en route to his mouth. "That can't be right. Who told you?"

"I found some things that made me wonder, and then Owen confirmed it." Jenny turned one of her blocks and picked up a spool of thread, spinning it on the table and setting it back down while she looked over the blocks.

"I guess I can understand. Working with family isn't for everyone. We've got a pretty unique business model here." Ron finally took a bite of his eclair.

Jenny let out a frustrated breath and picked up two different block configurations, one entirely made up of half square triangles, and one with full rectangles where each star leg ended snowballed.

"I just don't understand. I can't figure any of this out." She dropped the blocks and looked at the half-eaten eclair, not even wanting the last of it. "I try and understand what's going on, and everything keeps changing. But at the same time, nothing has. It's all the same."

Jenny waved a hand at the table, and Ron raised an eyebrow at the quilt blocks she'd upended in her deliberation.

"I don't think we're talking about your tutorial, are we? I don't even think we're talking about the business."

Jenny sank back in the chair and closed her eyes.

"I was only trying to help. I talked to everyone that was at the house the night of Mickey's murder. They still killed Lizzy. It may have been Sally. Sally may have killed her sister, Sally could still get killed. I saw how she reacted when we found Lizzy, and she wasn't faking that. I even had

Lizzy as one of the possible suspects." Jenny shook her head and grabbed the rest of the eclair. After she swallowed, she waved a hand at the quilt squares. "I just have no idea what I'm doing."

"Well, who's left?"

Ron's polite prodding did little to pull her out of her stress.

"You don't really want to talk about this," Jenny said softly. She hadn't meant to start ranting.

"No," Ron admitted. "But I know you, and you won't let it go till someone finds the truth. You have a good heart, Jenny. Just be careful. Can you promise me that?"

He took her hand, and Jenny gratefully took his in return.

"You know I'll try. Besides, all my suspects have been discounted. It just feels wrong."

"Like who?" Ron asked, and Jenny looked at him, gauging his words.

"Like Helen and Sally. Lizzy Rose is off the board for obvious reasons, and the other retreat guests were officially cleared. But while Helen and Sally are still there, I just can't imagine them doing this."

"Okay, so what do they have that makes them seem guilty?" Ron asked, mopping up the last of the cream and chocolate from the eclair plate with his finger.

A Body in Redwork

Jenny tried to remember. "Helen fought with Mickey. Mickey stole her line. She also paints similarly to the painter who is making the cards, but that's got to be a coincidence, right? Because Helen had the opportunity to step into Mickey's job and she wouldn't do it. Helen is also always trying to help. But Sally, she was basically being blackmailed by Mickey. Her relationship with Lizzy was being used against her. In order to keep it secret, they had to give Mickey whatever she wanted. The police say killing Lizzy was an accident, but I don't buy it. Harpers is also struggling financially. So I don't know if that makes them more or less likely to kill off their employees. The first poem referenced 'Striking the Harp' like Harper Wovens. But Sally and Owen are the only members of the team still in town and alive."

"And they're not designers," Ron said, cocking his head to the side and double-checking with Jenny. "Right? They're not, are they?"

"Not anymore. Owen never was, but Sally started off her career as a fabric designer."

"Didn't you say before that this is targeted at designers from Harper Wovens? That puts her in the limelight, doesn't it?"

"That's true, but other than Sally, I can't figure

out who is connected to both these women." Jenny leaned into her hand. The points of the star blocks on the table were all starting to blur. "People have done it before, but Sally?" Jenny could still see the tears on her face, and her gut tightened. "It couldn't be Sally."

"So what about Owen?" Ron asked like it was the obvious question, and considering the way he'd threatened her, she realized he was right..

"Owen definitely has a tie to both of them. I just have to wonder why. He seemed pretty upset at the thought of them being hurt but I suppose that's exactly what you'd do if you were guilty. It also seems like Mickey's death hasn't been all bad for the company."

"Sounds like similar motives as Sally's, right?" Ron eyed the empty plate and stood. He seemed grateful that Jenny had settled onto something. "Do you think anyone would notice if there was one less treat when we take them to the grandkids?"

"Not even a little." Jenny chuckled.

10

"You don't have to come if you don't want to." Jenny held a mascara wand to her lashes and looked over at Cherry as she adjusted her necklace in the mirror.

Thursday had come and almost gone. The designer's show had opened and no booths had collapsed, no more notes had been delivered. As Jenny swiped another coat of mascara on she was almost nervous to believe it. Outside, evening dimmed on Hamilton, Cherry and Jenny were getting ready for the swanky Meet and Greet that all the designers were supposed to be at.

"Oh, I'm coming. There's no way I'm letting you run off by yourself." Cherry grumpily checked herself in the mirror. Her muted yellow shift dress was accented with tangerine and aqua beads and projected a much brighter look than her expression. "Besides, the flowers came in and the decor is done.

So I'm ready to enjoy myself. As long as you can leave this searching-for-bad-guys thing at home. You need to be careful."

"I am careful." Jenny finished her eyes and touched up her lips. Her own outfit was somewhat more understated than Cherry's. The navy-blue slacks were paired with a deep blush blouse. The tunic style top had just a hint of sparkle at the neckline, and she'd found a matching navy cardigan that looked perfect with the set.

"You're right. You look great. You're going to be fine." Cherry smiled brightly and forced the next words through her teeth. "I can't believe we're doing this."

"Cherry!" Jenny pushed her out the door.

"It's a good thing there's going to be cake." Cherry moved down the hall and descended the stairs to where Ron waited. "And handsome men." Cherry wiggled her eyebrows at Jenny.

Ron looked great. As he offered Jenny his arm, she found she didn't mind the teasing at all.

"I'll take this handsome man. You can have the rest."

Cherry rolled her eyes.

"I'm thrilled to be with two such beautiful ladies." Ron opened the door, his eyes resting on Jenny. "You look wonderful."

A Body in Redwork

"A person could drown in all this sweetness." Cherry pushed past them, making her way to the car.

Ron held the door for Jenny. "You look amazing tonight. But you do every night. I'd love to sit by you if you have room."

She kissed him, grateful to have him at her side.

The three of them arrived at the Meet and Greet with time to spare. The party was being held at a new event center at the edge of town. They'd decorated the brick building with strings of antique light bulbs and filled the flower beds with huge fronds of grasses and little spots of color. The grasses flanked large glass doors under a porch-sized awning suspended by metal cables.

The rest of the retreat group was already waiting at the center. Bernie and Dotty stood by the front doors in matching pantsuits. Dotty's was a forest green and Bernie wore deep red with a jeweled wreath brooch on her blouse. Tilly had a hold of Maura's arm, the two of them giggling over every sew-lebrity that passed by. As the youngest of the group, the two women wore distinctly different levels of formal wear. While Maura carried her jeans and Christmas sweater off with all the confidence of a rock star, Tilly was decked out in a sparkling dress and what looked like Christmas ornaments hanging from her ears.

Jenny stepped onto the sidewalk and jumped when Helen joined them.

"I didn't see you," Jenny said. "I'm actually a little surprised to see you. How are you feeling?"

"I didn't want to stay home alone." Helen tucked her hair behind her ears and tugged at the sides of her pencil skirt, like she was trying too hard to be comfortable.

Jenny put an arm around her as they followed the group into the building. Tables edged the large main hall, with quilted valances strung decoratively through the lighting and greenery along the exposed brick walls. The women drifted into the large group of designers, fabric manufacturers, shop owners, and wide-eyed quilters, everyone bundled in nerves and excitement.

With the dim lights and fancy decor, it felt a little like a grown-up prom. The only thing missing was the awkward dancing and a corner photo booth.

"Look, Jenny." Cherry pointed to the far side of the hall.

There were stand-up figures of herself and many of the designers next to a three-paneled display, encrusted with cutouts of the Missouri Star Quilt Company logo in a variety of sizes. If quilt blocks could sparkle, these stars were doing their best work.

A Body in Redwork

"We can check photo booth off the list." Jenny shook her head, not sure if she should laugh or hide.

"Let's take a photo with you."

Jenny steered her away. "Oh, trust me, it's been done."

She headed to the opposite side of the hall.

"Without me?" Cherry sounded appalled.

Jenny let out a breath. "Check with Natalie. She saves all the good pictures."

Cherry burst out in laughter. "Oh, I will!"

Jenny didn't love that Cherry was so amused by this idea.

Tilly and Maura had found a table, and many of their friends had joined them. Cherry followed reluctantly.

"Hello, ladies. It's nice to see you again." Hugo shook their hands as they settled in at the large booth and waited for the obligatory admiration.

"Oh, my goodness," Maura gushed, and Hugo turned. "I love your work. I've kept fat quarter sets of all your lines. Your first three were my absolute favorite."

"You liked my beginning lines?" Hugo's grin faded. "You know I'm still designing, right?"

"Of course," Maura giggled.

Hugo glanced down at them, then looked beyond their table. "You'll have to let me know what you think when you get to my recent work. I hope you all have a lovely evening." With a smooth sweep of his arms, he stepped away from the table.

"Hello. Don't you women look beautiful tonight?" he said to the next group.

"Oh. Did I say something wrong?" Maura stared after her design hero, her jaw hanging open.

"No," Jenny said. "He's just trying to find as many admirers as he can."

Maura stared at him where he was talking to the next table. "Well, I can't imagine Harper Wovens designers being that abrupt."

"He has his own label." Cherry pursed her lips as she stared after the man. "He's not moving to Harpers."

"You haven't seen his social media posts, have you?" Maura turned her attention to her friends. "He posts little Harpers shout-outs on a regular basis. And once over a year ago he had a blip of a story that was all about how if he could work for anyone, it would be Harpers."

"I didn't know that." Jenny watched him move onto the next table. Everyone had dreams. Maybe that was why he was always popping up at the Harper Wovens booth.

The evening turned to joking and food. After a while, someone announced the designers would be stationed at tables around the room. Within seconds, Cherry and Jenny were the only ones left sitting at their table. Their friends all dispersed into the crowd.

"Well, Ms. Carmine, I guess I better go." Jenny smiled, and Ron held out his hand to help her up.

"Alright, Mrs. Doan. I'll be mingling with some famous person. Don't mind me."

Jenny had no doubt Cherry would meet every designer in the house.

"I'll be over there. Let me know if you hear anything interesting."

Cherry tipped her head to the side, an eyebrow raised high. "Like what?"

"Oh, confessions to various crimes, insinuation of guilt, or a love of Sally Harpers scarves."

Cherry nearly choked on her Apple Core Template-tini mocktail. "Scarves? You must think I'm going to go around interrogating people."

"No," Jenny drew the word out and raised a hand in a theatrical display of disagreement. "You could keep your ears and eyes open, though."

Jenny pointed to her own ears and then to Cherry, as if to tell her she better be listening. Cherry pulled both hands up as if she didn't understand, and turned away with a smile on her face.

Jenny perused the room, stopping to greet many

of the designers. As she passed the table where the Pears & Gin designers were visiting with guests, Maggie Sun waved and excused herself.

"How are you? Ruby told me what happened. I just can't believe I didn't realize what had happened." Maggie's wide eyed concern felt syrupy sweet.

Thanking her for her concern, Jenny caught sight of some of her friends and excused herself. Pausing to get a drink she joined Maura and Tilly leaning together near Vana Suze's table.

"Did you see the pictures of her new studio?" Maura asked, looking past Jenny at Vana Suze.

Tilly grabbed Maura's elbow. "Umm, yes! It's gorgeous, isn't it?" Tilly raved about the rows of fabric shelves. "But my favorite will always be Sally Harpers. Have you seen how she organizes it? Everything's in rainbow color. It just makes my heart happy."

"Do you think those two will ever get together?" Maura asked absently, scanning the designers at the various tables.

"What two?" Jenny felt more than a little lost stepping into their conversation. The two women followed so many designers she didn't know how they kept everyone straight.

"Owen Teak and Sally Harper," Tilly said.

"There've been rumors going around about them forever. How can you work together for so long and not either love or hate the other person?"

"And they don't seem to hate each other. But . . ." Maura tipped her drink toward the Harper Wovens booth where Owen stood alone. "Owen is usually dating someone else."

Tilly shook her head. "But he's always so sweet and protective of Sally. There's got to be something there."

Jenny knew first-hand how protective of Sally he was, and the memory made her anxious. "It's really none of our business."

Maura shrugged. "I know. But watching Sally post about how great their team is and the nice things he's done makes you wonder. Maybe she has a crush on Owen."

"She posted the other day that he'd bought her flowers." Tilly scrolled through her phone and flashed open the screen.

It was the Amaryllis. Jenny's confusion on that silly plant was not the kind of road block she'd been planning on. Had Owen bought it? And who added the card? For all Jenny knew, it could have been added later.

"It's silly, but being a designer just seems so glamorous. Even with everything going on, I'm glad to be here. Tonight has been surreal." Maura looked around the room enamored with all the design royalty.

Jenny's skin warmed, and she worried she was going to get splotchy. Tipping her head, she sought out any of the other girls who'd come with them. "I'm just glad to be with my friends. I can't imagine having all of this happen without you guys there to support me."

"I feel the same way. I can't imagine hearing about Mickey and being across the country. I'd have come right away," Maura said.

Tilly leaned against the table, her eyes telling the same story. Maura waved her hand around, drawing them back into the party. "And don't worry, we aren't going to do anything embarrassing. We promise."

Tilly smirked. "No guarantees. There will be dancing. And I might fall in love with Owen Teak before the night's through. Unless I can get him to fall first."

"We have one night," Maura laughed. "May the best woman win."

Tilly giggled and covered her mouth. But when Maura joined in, their laughter grew boisterous enough that they drew the attention of the neighboring tables and passing quilters.

A Body in Redwork

Tilly waved a hand. "Don't tell me you would give up Hugo Hensen for Owen?"

"Hmm . . . he's still handsome, but after tonight I'd say I have an opening for a favorite designer."

"Owen's not a designer," Jenny said.

"Details." Maura took a drink as if she didn't care. But a second later she shot a long glance over to Hugo's table where he was surrounded by guests.

Behind Hugo, a tall blonde leaned in to say something. He smiled and nodded, but as she walked away, Hugo glared after her.

When the woman turned, Jenny's breath caught. Sally Harper was making her way back to the Harper Wovens corner of the room.

"Girls." Jenny reached out and squeezed their hands in lieu of a real goodbye. "I wish you both luck on your designer search. I'll see you tonight, okay?" Jenny didn't wait for a response before pushing away from the table.

Sally passed the Pears & Gin booth, and Jenny hurried to catch her. Jenny skirted a large table, garnering a few raised eyebrows as she tried to cut Sally off.

"Sally," Jenny called as they passed the side door.

Sally stepped up to Owen at their table. He looked behind her toward Jenny. Jenny stumbled backward, hiding behind a plant. After their last

conversation, she didn't feel like confronting Owen.
The side door stood open into a courtyard behind
her. Jenny peaked around the plant and saw Owen
arguing with Sally. He lifted his eyes and spotted
her.

Jenny hurried outside behind a couple of friends
chatting about the latest quilting trends. She sat at
one of the tables worrying that Owen would make
good on his threat and not let her near Sally. How
would she help prove Sally's innocence if she
couldn't even talk to her?

"Harper Wovens has got to be doing better than
ever after Mickey Steven's designs went crazy like
that."

The voices behind Jenny hadn't gotten any
louder, but the use of her friend's name caught her
attention.

Jenny glanced back. The garden was lit overhead
with string lights and vintage bulbs, with
strategically placed plants creating little alcoves and
privacy. The women were facing the garden,
partially hidden behind a particularly large potted
plant. They probably didn't even realize she was
there.

"I could only order half the line for my shop."
"Wow."
The first woman's shock echoed Jenny's

thoughts. The page with the sales printout flashed in her mind.

"I guess they're all limited editions now," the woman continued. "Do you think they'll reprint?"

Jenny didn't hear the next part, as Owen walked past the doorway inside the event center. Jenny pushed her chair back and stood. Sally would be alone now.

A second chair scratched against the ground, and behind her someone called out. "Jenny Doan?" the taller of the women asked.

Her friend smacked her shoulder lightly. "She's obviously taking a break. I'm sorry, Jenny. I'm Kim and this is Leslie. We're big fans. But we don't want to bother you."

"Could we just maybe get one picture?" Leslie glanced at her friend nervously, already working her phone to the right screen in case Jenny agreed.

"Of course." Jenny glanced back at the doorway. "I would love to. How about over here? The garden is so beautiful."

The women moved together in the little alcove where they'd been visiting and faced away from the garden so it could be in the picture. As they set up the shot, Jenny caught a glimpse of Owen inside the room, glancing back toward Harpers. Maggie followed after him, and Jenny's eyes widened.

Jenny's new friends snapped the picture.

She was going to look ridiculous.

Jenny didn't care. It could be their internet sensation.

"Thanks so much!" Jenny said, and gave them both hugs before hurrying away.

Owen had disappeared again by the time she got through the door, and Maggie with him. Jenny bit her lip, not sure if she should try and follow him. When she saw Sally standing alone at the Harper Wovens table, she made up her mind.

Jenny grabbed her friend in a hug. "I can't believe you're here! What did the police say? I thought you'd still be with them."

"It's fine, sort of. Okay, it's not fine, but I have no idea what to do. Thank goodness Owen vouched for my whereabouts, or I might have been kept. But I'm worried it won't hold up, considering we're so close. They said they have evidence that puts me at the crime scenes, but I didn't kill my sister or Mickey. Why would I do that?"

Sally was gripping the table, which Jenny saw as a good thing, since any time she let go, Sally's hands flew out in exaggerated emphasis of whatever she was saying. Sally dropped her face into her hands.

Jenny patted her back and tried to console her.

A Body in Redwork

"Maybe they consider the increase in sales as motive, but it's not something you can do anything about."

"What are you talking about? Nothing has changed in our sales. Mickey is gone, Liz is gone. Owen told me last night he's working on some ideas. Hugo is the last one on the collaboration team. I'm having to call up old friends and I'm trying to fill the gap myself. As if I didn't have enough things to worry about." Sally straightened and pulled her hair back, the Harper Wovens pin on her lapel glinting under the lights.

Jenny couldn't decide if Sally was lying or being lied to, but she gestured to the pin. "I know this is hard, but, Sally, you're doing amazing things. Look at that pin. It looks great on you."

Sally's brows pinched in confusion, and her hand went to her chest where the pin was tacked to her shirt. "Oh, this? It's not mine. It's Lizzy's. After I went home last night, I found her pin on the dresser. She was always forgetting to wear it to events." Sally rubbed her fingers over the yellow enamel. "Probably 'cause she didn't even want to be a Harpers designer."

"That's Lizzy's pin?" Jenny didn't want to make things more painful, but she was certain Lizzy had been wearing it. "You were sharing a room, right?

Couldn't it have been yours?"

"I don't have one. I wasn't a designer anymore when we started making them. I have extras, but they're with our supplies. So, yeah, it's hers."

"But Lizzy was wearing her pin. At the park when we found her. It was pinned to her blouse."

Sally's fingers pinched the pin as she twisted the button and took it off. "That's impossible. This was hers. I found it on Lizzy's dresser after they released me."

Sally turned the pin in her fingers, and Jenny turned the idea in her mind.

"So someone gave her a new pin?" Jenny said.

"I guess so, but what's the purpose in that?" Sally looked at Jenny with all the confusion of a new quilter contemplating the Mariners Star.

"The only reason to wear one would be to identify them as Harper Wovens designers, right? So really, it seems like the murderer is targeting your company."

Sally blanched, and the pin dropped to the table, spinning in tiny circles across the black cloth. "I killed them."

11

Jenny caught Lizzy's pin and handed it back to her friend. The exclamation was extreme and dramatic. Jenny could feel Sally's need to have her innocence validated.

"Sally, this is not your fault." Was it? She didn't want to ask the question, but it hung on her lips. With every tearful confession and every astonished response, Jenny was beginning to wonder why so many signs pointed to Sally.

"No. I know you're right. I just feel so upset. I didn't—"

"What's Owen doing with Maggie? I thought they were done." Hugo cut into the conversation appearing out of nowhere.

Sally's mouth dropped open and closed like a fish. "They, umm, they are, or were. What are they doing?"

Hugo smiled like he and Sally were best friends.

Sally gripped the edge of her table so hard Jenny suspected her knuckles were turning white.

It was the first time Jenny had seen Hugo act so natural, which made the whole interaction feel oddly unnatural. "Sneaking off to dark rooms. Looking into each other's eyes. You know the drill."

Sally's mouth dropped open. She absently wiped at one of her red eyes, then pressed her hand over her mouth. "He told me they were done. He was helping me. He told me he would be here for me. Are you sure?"

Hugo held up his hands. "Hey, I'm just asking. I thought you should know if you two were getting together."

"I can't believe he would do this to me. Not now when I need him so much." Sally's voice lowered. "It won't last. Maggie's going to be gone soon."

Hugo glanced at Jenny as if just noticing her and took a step back. "I'll see you later, Sally."

Sally handed Jenny one of the fabric cards. "I have to go . . . and I don't think I'll be back tonight. But I'll see you in the morning, right? At the booth?"

"I didn't think—Owen said—" Jenny's confusion was cut off when Sally waved a hand.

"It starts at noon." Sally hurried across the floor

and bumped into a waiter on her way out. She didn't look back.

Cherry walked up slowly, watching Sally disappear into the crowd. "What was that?"

Jenny shook her head. "I think Sally is in love with Owen."

"Well, yeah. Anyone with eyes could tell you that." Cherry scanned the list she'd prepped for the evening. "Where do you think I'll find Vana Suze?"

"You knew? I wonder how long it's been one-sided." Jenny had lost sight of Sally but couldn't help wondering if her issues with the women designers was simple jealousy. She handed Cherry the card of fabric samples. "Here. Watch the table. I'll be right back."

"But—Jenny. Where are you going? Jenny." Cherry hissed. Jenny slipped away through the crowd and behind her she heard Cherry's voice change. "Oh, hey, Ron. You brought cookies. How sweet."

Jenny glanced back. Cherry was busy turning Ron away from where she'd gone. As Cherry walked Ron across the floor, he looked back several times, and Cherry pointed toward the wall. Jenny said a little prayer of gratitude for Cherry and her loyalty and hurried after Sally.

People and decor were everywhere as Jenny

stumbled through the event center in a haze. Normally she loved the bustle of a party, but tonight the noise was overwhelming. Every so often she would hear her name, and she'd smile and wave, but thankfully the guests were here to meet designers. Jenny had been so close to being that person tonight. But after the conversations she'd had with Sally, she had more questions than answers.

Jenny pushed through the main doors, plunging into the night air. The parking lot was empty. She let the doors close behind her and circled carefully among the cars. Sally was nowhere. Jenny had either gone the wrong way or she'd been too slow.

Jenny made her way back to the building and opened the doors. She gave a startled yell when she walked right into herself.

A lifesize Jenny Doan standee was tipped across an entry table, her hand raised and blocking the door. Jenny, the real Jenny, almost tripped under her own arm. Ignoring the laughter and chatter, Jenny lifted the standup image of herself onto its feet and slid it back to its place beside the table where it could wave to people as they left.

She leaned against the coat closet behind the figure and let the giggles die down. She needed to think. She gripped the door knob of the coat closet and paused. Someone was already in there.

A Body in Redwork

"You know that's not what I meant. I just want to know why your paintings are police evidence?"

The ominous question pulled Jenny closer. The only paintings she knew of that were police evidence were the ones on the notecards. Her fingers twitched on the doorknob. If she opened it and startled them, she could find out who it was. But then they could get away. Jenny's hand twitched toward her phone before she remembered she didn't have it with her. She'd given it to Ron to hold since her current dress had no pockets. She knew better than to wear dresses without pockets.

"What makes you think they're mine?"

"I recognized your signature. I know you painted those cards, and the police are going to figure it out sooner than later."

Jenny held her breath. This was dangerous. She heard two people, a man and a woman. Someone needed to know if one of them was a possible killer. But the voices were so familiar. She leaned closer, her face pressed against the wooden door frame.

The crowd behind her was busy talking and laughing, but even in a party it wouldn't take long to notice the six-foot-tall face of the Missouri Star Quilt Company eavesdropping on the coat closet. She needed more time. Jenny grabbed the standee of herself and casually dragged it over a few feet to block the closet door.

"Your paintings have been at both murders. And the girls were painted to match the creepy dolls you put in the card."

"You say that like my artwork killed them. I mean, I'm good, but I'm not that good." The woman's voice was resonant and warm . . . and defensive. "I make cards and sell them online. I'm trying to make a little extra money. So sue me. Anyone could have bought them. Besides, I don't have any pieces with dolls on them."

"Well, someone added them." The man sounded annoyed. Jenny could relate. If someone had added the dolls after the fact it could have been the artist he was talking to or anyone else. Except, they'd done a very good job of adding them. It was a smooth enough change that even seeing them in person, she hadn't realized they'd been added.

"Well, there you have it. I guess I didn't kill anyone."

Jenny didn't trust the voice.

"Maggie."

Jenny blinked, stunned by the revelation and instantly recognizing Owen's voice with hers. Could Maggie Sun be the artist? Owen's strange reaction to the cards the night before suddenly made sense. He'd lied about recognizing them and had come straight to Maggie. It seemed to eliminate him, but Maggie hadn't even been on Jenny's list. She wondered if the police knew about Owen and Maggie's previous relationship, since neither he nor Sally seemed to want to talk about it.

"Look, I don't know what your problem is. This is making your life better, isn't it? More money, old girlfriends disappearing. It's what you wanted, right? I don't see the problem." Maggie's confusion opened a new view of the case.

Jenny pulled back. This was news.

She needed to find Ron or Cherry or anyone with a phone.

"The problem could be that you're also an 'old' girlfriend. Or did you not consider that?"

Jenny couldn't decide if it was a threat or a warning.

"Maybe I'm just not worried about it. Sally doesn't see me as a threat."

Someone shuffled inside the closet, and Jenny backed up, bumping into the cardboard figure standing guard behind her.

"Why should we worry about Sally?" Owen asked. "Are you still holding a grudge against us? I can't help it. I run a company with her."

It was quiet for a moment. When Maggie finally

answered, it wasn't sad exactly, but maybe let down. "But it's still an 'us,' you and Sally?"

"It will be 'us' for a while." Owen sounded exasperated. "Until I figure out how to leave."

"Then I guess we've got nothing else to talk about."

"Come on."

"Sally destroyed my work when I applied there. If someone's cleaning out your team, you know it's Sally."

"Sally's harmless."

The door handle jiggled. Jenny jumped back, stumbling and knocking over the standee as the door opened.

Jenny looked up as Maggie walked out of the closet. She walked quickly back to her table not paying attention to anyone. Jenny stepped back, still struggling with the tipping cardboard cut out.

Cherry's hand grabbed the edge, and she helped Jenny heft it upright.

"There you are," Cherry said, taking the real Jenny's elbow and walking with her to the nearest table. "Ron has been wandering around with a handful of little cookies for you. And you're hiding behind yourself. Just don't tell me you've taken any more selfies without me."

"Shh," Jenny said, glancing at the closet door.

174

A Body in Redwork

Only a few seconds later, it opened, and Owen appeared, his eyes on everything. Including them. When he locked onto her, he stiffened and glared. Jenny looked away. Yup, he was still mad.

Cherry's hands fluttered, eyes wide with apology, and her accent grew heavy. "I'm so sorry. I had no idea we were spying. What did Owen do? I thought you were joking when you told me to watch out for criminals."

"I was. Well, kind of. But don't worry. I wasn't really spying. I was looking for someone." Jenny followed Owen's path across the floor.

"Owen?" Cherry asked, her voice a very pointed whisper. "Is he the killer?"

"I don't think so. But he and Maggie were talking about the murders in there, along with who knows what before I got there."

"Maggie? Sun?" Cherry looked back to the Pears & Gin booth and let out a low whistle. "I thought he and Sally were a thing. Any juicy news I should know about?"

"Juicy?" Jenny asked. Cherry regularly surprised Jenny by the things that came out of her mouth. "Apparently, she painted the notecards. Is that juicy?"

Cherry's lips popped open to form an O. "That's pretty juicy. And Owen is involved how?"

"I don't think it's Owen. He's just a flirt and he's upset, but it sounds like Sally gets jealous of anyone Owen is involved with. At this point, it's more likely to be her than him."

"You think it's Sally?"

"I've been wondering."

"And you're going to tell the police?" Cherry asked.

Jenny nodded. "I'll tell the police and I'm out."

"Good for you." Cherry lifted a mocktail from the tray of a passing waiter.

Jenny found one for herself before clinking glasses and sipping at the brightly colored liquid. Now that she knew they were additions to finished paintings, she wondered if she'd be able to tell the artist of the dolls.

Jenny gave a side glance to Cherry. "I may ask to see the notecards one more time."

Jenny stood under the streetlights outside the Sewing Center, her phone pressed to her ear.

Officer Wilkins' voice had turned somewhat mechanical after her many questions. "This is not a library. You can't simply check out evidence if you're not a police officer."

Jenny groaned as he explained again why the department wouldn't let her physically see the greeting cards she'd discovered.

"If I tell you who painted them, will you let me see them?"

"We also aren't an estate auction where you can bid for evidence. Mrs. Doan, if you know something about a current investigation and you don't tell us, you're withholding evidence and could be placed under arrest. I don't want to do that." Wilkins sounded exhausted.

Calling the police had seemed like a good idea before Wilkins started telling her all the reasons why she couldn't see the cards.

Cherry sat on the steps to the building as Jenny filled Officer Wilkins in on the financial motives of Harper Wovens, Owen's possible connection to the girls, and Maggie's definite connection to the cards.

A car honked, and the well-dressed quilters climbed out, their faces glowing with the excitement of the evening.

Cherry jumped up and bounced on the balls of her feet as the women climbed the steps to the raised sidewalk. Jenny hung up with Wilkins and turned to Cherry as their friends joined them.

"You're too excited. What's going on?"

Cherry giggled and sought out Helen in the crowd. "Let us in, Helen, because I have a surprise for everyone and I can't wait for you to see it!"

Helen unlocked the door, and Cherry led the way up the stairs.

"You're going to love it. All the flowers made it in this afternoon, and I set up while everyone was getting ready, before the event. I hope having the sewing room unavailable wasn't a problem."

Amid nods and laughter the women made it up the steps. Cherry grabbed the door handle and turned around, holding them back. "So it's a little different. I took Andi's garland down, but we don't have to tell her yet. It just looks so good like this."

Jenny couldn't help smiling. "I'm not telling her."

Bernie pushed her way forward. "We've got your back, Cherry. Now let's go inside. I want to sit down."

"Okay, okay. Welcome to the Winter Redwork Retreat." Cherry twisted the knob and pushed the door open.

Bernie went through first. "Oh thank goodness. I need to sit down—Oh."

Maura was right on her heels, and her gasp was immediate. Stopping in the doorway. Cherry turned, anxious to get everyone inside. She slid next to Maura, all the while telling them about her favorite parts of the decor.

"I've got fabric garlands up to accent the red florals in white pots. Against the white walls, I just love—" Cherry stopped in her tracks as she made it through the crowd of women.

She didn't move, and Jenny squeezed between Maura and Bernie to see what had stopped them. Jenny inhaled an involuntary gasp as the room came into view.

"What happened?" Tilly pushed them even farther into the room.

"I don't know." Cherry moved to a table, where an amaryllis plant lay broken.

The entire place had been destroyed. Plants that had been a staple of Cherry's design were uprooted and thrown to the ground. Sewing supplies were scattered across tables, and Jenny's entire sewing table had been upended, machine and supplies dumped to the ground. Taped to the underside of the table was a little red envelope.

Jenny pulled it off the table and held it up for Cherry to see. "This is not good."

Cherry took the card and removed a hand-painted red card from the envelope. "It's another poem. 'Have Yourself a Merry Little Christmas.'"

"Read it," Jenny said. She wanted to take it back. She didn't want to know what it said.

"I can't. I don't know the song that well."

Jenny stared at her.

"Seriously? You don't have to sing it." She took the note back from Cherry.

Have yourself a little care this Christmas.
Help your fears alight.
Know that I have seen you
      meddling through the night.
If there's those who are dear to you,
Gathered near to you, observe.
Stop seeking for my truth to find
Or your life is mine, reserved.

Keep your friends and all of those who love you,
By forgetting me.
Or someone you need will take their final bow.

So, Jenny, you should take a little care right now.

Jenny stared at the words. "That's the most elaborate 'back off' I've ever heard."

Cherry snatched the card from her grip and glared at it. She flipped the cover closed then open, reading it over, the whole time shaking her head.

"Well, you got your wish. Now you can see the card up close and in person. Do you want to call Tyler or should I?"

"Call him." Jenny looked at the card. "It doesn't have a dolly anyway."

"Of course, she wants the card people get because they're dead. Super. Let's hope for that one." Cherry started setting flower pots upright.

Dotty came over, worry pulling her brows into a tight pinch behind her glasses. "Jenny, who would do this? I don't want anyone else to die."

Jenny shook her head. "People are trying to be intimidating. That's all."

Cherry pulled Jenny aside, "I know they weren't part of the threat when it was Harper designers that were being targeted, but this note specifically said they're targeting your friends and family. Look around you. This group is entirely your friends. You may not be worried, but they are."

Maura and Tilly were picking up chunks of broken pottery while Bernie and Helen swept and Dotty picked up sewing supplies. Cherry nudged Jenny forward.

"Hey everyone. I'm so sorry that you've gotten dragged into this. I want you to know that I'm planning to leave this to the police. I love you all and I don't want to be the reason that any of you get hurt."

Dotty looked across the room at Bernie, and Maura shook her head. "We don't want you to stop."

Cherry's gaze snapped to Maura.

Tilly bit her lip. "Someone needs to stop him. Jenny, if you've got whoever it is this scared, you must be on the right track."

"We'll be fine, Jenny. Just let them try and take on all of us."

Cherry's jaw hit the floor. "You can't be serious." The women all looked at her and Cherry brushed her hands together as if shaking them off. "Fine. But you need to call Tyler." She held out her phone. "Officer Wilkins needs to know that everyone here has been threatened. And they don't care one bit."

Jenny took the phone and Cherry walked out of the room.

Jenny followed her out the door. Cherry was shaking her head. "You should be quilting. Don't you have a video to film on Friday?"

"Yeah, but we've got to catch a killer first. I don't plan to do it by myself. But if we don't, he goes home with the designers and gets away with all of it."

Cherry clutched the card. Her mouth worked open and closed as if she was looking for something to say, something to explain her worry. "What if we don't?"

Jenny's chest contracted at the thought. "We will."

12

Light streamed through the windows over the guest beds in Cherry and Jenny's room. Cherry groaned and pulled a pillow over her head.

"Why is the sun shining?"

"It's not." Jenny rolled over, peeking at her friend through slitted eyes. "Go back to bed."

It had been a long night of cleaning up dirt and decorations, and yet people were already moving around in the hallway.

"Somebody's up." Cherry sat up in bed and squinted at the door. "Who's awake out there?"

"Hello?" an unfamiliar voice called.

Jenny sat up, and both women looked at each other, suddenly wide awake.

"Just a minute," Jenny called back as the two women rushed around getting into presentable clothing.

Jenny stepped out of the room with Cherry hurrying after her. She closed the door and smiled at a couple not much older than she was. The woman had Mickey's coloring with red hair and freckles and the man carried several of Mickey's suitcases with him.

"Hi, I'm Jenny Doan." Jenny held out her hand to greet the couple.

"Oh good," the woman said, clasping Jenny's hand. "I think we're looking for you. We're Michelle, er, Mickey's parents." Tears welled in the woman's eyes as she took Jenny's hand and fought to control herself. The man pulled her close and she crumpled against him.

Jenny looked between them as Mrs. Stevens stopped crying.

"I'm sorry." She muttered, staring at the floor now. "It's so terrible, and even saying her name, I just . . . I can't." Her lip quivered even getting through that much of her speech.

"You're the Stevenses." Jenny shook Mr. Stevens' hand and put her arm around Mrs. Stevens' shoulders. "Come this way."

Jenny moved ahead leading them toward the sewing room. "We aren't in our normal setup here, but I'd love to have you sit down for a moment. We're all so sad about Mickey."

Helen's head poked out of her door as Jenny ushered the couple into the corner room. The large windows that lined the front and side wall still held a smattering of dirt. Somehow Andi had already discovered the mishap and was sweeping up the remains of what they'd missed the night before.

A Body in Redwork

"Oh, amaryllis are so beautiful." Mickey's mother sat next to the one remaining plant on the end table near a hard-backed chair.

"We had a lot more last night," Cherry said. She held two cups of tea in her hands and offered them to the group.

Mrs. Stevens declined and looked at Cherry with furrowed brows. When neither of their guests accepted the tea, Cherry gave one of the steaming cups to Jenny, then settled in with the group.

"We actually stopped by to say thank you for always hosting Mickey and being so kind."

"Mickey was a dear friend. She had so much going for her. I'm so sorry that she was taken the way she was." Jenny stumbled over her words. She couldn't imagine having to collect her child's things after they'd died, much less been killed.

"She was. And she always looked forward to spending time with your group. She talked about this trip for months. I can't believe it. I just wish we knew what happened."

"Everyone is working really hard to figure out who did this. Mickey shouldn't have died."

Mrs. Stevens started crying and Jenny reached over taking her hands while Mr. Stevens tucked her under his arm again. She leaned against her husband and Jenny squeezed her hand while she squeezed back.

"I wish there was anything we could do to help. I just don't know. They didn't let us take anything with us." Jenny looked to Cherry, whose eyes were red as she watched the tortured couple.

"Did Mickey have siblings?" Cherry asked. "Maybe we could send some flowers with you for everyone."

Mr. Stevens smiled. "She did. But they don't need flowers. They just want the memories, and we've already got those."

Mrs. Stevens sniffled.

"I'm so sorry for your loss." Jenny watched their glistening eyes. Even Mr. Stevens who hadn't cried openly here had a sheen of emotion across his eyes. "Mickey was always so kind and generous."

"Oh, speaking of that, we came to retrieve her things and there were several boxes I thought your group might enjoy." Mr. Stevens unzipped one of the cases he was carrying. "It's the main reason we stopped by."

He unloaded several boxes. One was the engraved walnut seam rippers and the next was gold-trimmed walnut needle cases. All the delicate little tools sat in neat rows marked with a little engraving of "Love, Mickey".

Jenny lifted one out of the box and turned the tool around in her hand.

Mr. Stevens puffed up a little. "Pretty things, aren't they?"

Jenny smiled and replaced it in the box. Mr. Stevens shifted the boxes toward them. "She would have wanted you to have them."

"These are gorgeous." Jenny couldn't help reaching out to touch them. They really were stunning. "Mickey outdid herself. She must have spent a fortune."

"Oh, just the extra trim pieces. All the wood was down on the property, and she had cheap labor." He winked, setting the little case in line with the others.

"Are you saying you made these?"

"Michelle and I did 'em." Mr. Stevens grinned, pushing his hands against his knees and making room for his chest to inflate a little farther.

Jenny couldn't believe it. "I had no idea Mickey was this kind of creative."

"Oh, yes." Mrs. Stevens answered this time with a firm nod of her head. "She loved wood-working with her dad. They made things like this every year. And since there wasn't much money to be had, it was convenient that hand carvings were her activity of choice. Well, until last year. She worked these in, but last year she spent almost the whole time working on her fabric line. With her friends helping her, she was finally able to get it done."

Mrs. Stevens touched the edge of the suitcase, rubbing at the name tag that hung from the handle.

Jenny leaned forward, and held Mrs. Stevens gaze through her glistening tears. "I have loved knowing Mickey. I am so sorry for your pain and for your loss. Thank you for sharing her with us."

"She wasn't the kind of person to hide away. Wasn't meant for that. I'm just grateful she was finally happy. What with us losing the house and all, I worried for a while that she was going to fall apart." Mr. Stevens took his wife's hand, and she looked up at him sadly.

"I didn't know. Is there anything we can do?"

"Oh, we didn't lose the house. Michelle saved it. She got a huge advance on the fabric line she sold and started sending us regular installments. This whole thing was such a blessing until—" Mr. Stevens stopped and looked at his wife.

"Until now," Mrs. Stevens finished for him.

Mickey must have received quite a large chunk of money to be able to do that, and it wouldn't have been a fabric advance. This was why Mickey did it. She sold the line and blackmailed friends to save her family. It wasn't right.

Jenny's heart ached that Mickey had thought that was the only way.

Mr. and Mrs. Stevens stood to leave, and Jenny hugged them both.

"Mickey loved you so much," Mrs. Stevens said.

"I am so glad we got to meet you. We'll make sure the girls get these gifts from Mickey."

Something crashed to the ground by the window, and the small crew turned at the sound. Andi dropped to the ground and scooped up whatever had fallen. Ducking her head, she started toward the door.

"Sorry, I'll just be a minute," Andi said as she hurried to the door.

Mr. Stevens put out a hand, stopping her. He looked closely at her face. "Andrea?"

Andi's face blanched. She shook her head and bolted from the room.

A Body in Redwork

Jenny had to check several rooms before she found Andi in one of the last bedrooms, sitting on an unmade bed. She sat leaning back against the wall, fiddling with something in her hand. Andi glanced up as Jenny came inside.

"Andrea?" Jenny asked.

Andi nodded, and turned something over in her fingers.

"You knew Mickey?"

Andi nodded again and looked away. The thing in her hand was the charm bracelet, and Andi sat flipping the charms between her fingers. "I knew her. Not well, but I knew her."

"You want to tell me about it?" Jenny had worked with a lot of scared kids and right then, despite her experience and her age, Andi felt like a scared kid.

Andi wouldn't look at Jenny. She fiddled with the bracelet and looked anywhere in the room besides at Jenny. Jenny waited.

Andi closed her eyes, and the words came out. "Mickey was always one of the nice ones. When she found out I wanted to design fabric she suggested we work together. All last summer we worked on art and fine-tuned pieces and tried to get ourselves together. Mickey always said that was her problem: she couldn't get her act together to finish a project.

191

And like she said, somewhere in the middle she fizzled out."

"But Mickey sold her line. Did you know Mickey had finished?"

But Mickey hadn't finished. She must have gotten together with Helen during that time and realized she could use Helen's rejected artwork. Jenny amended her questions.

"Did you know she was submitting to fabric companies without you? That must have been really frustrating."

"It was. But I was also really happy for her. I found out when I saw her name on our lists for the designers convention. She quit talking to me after she sold her line I guess. It was last summer some time and all of a sudden she was gone. I didn't know what happened except that she'd left me too."

Jenny could imagine that Mickey probably got so caught up in keeping track of her lies that she couldn't keep up with her friends. But she didn't want to say that, not with the trauma it had created here. "I'm sure she just got busy."

"Of course she did. It's great to have a friend when they're helping you, but as soon as you're done, you move on, right?" Andi clenched her fist around the little charms. One of them stuck out between her fingers, a yellow circle with Harper Wovens Designer written around the edge.

Only one person would have a charm like that. It was the same charm Jenny had seen on the bracelet

Andi had been wearing earlier that week, on the day Mickey died.

"Is that Mickey's charm bracelet?" Jenny asked, scooting over to the edge of the bed and pointing to the charm.

Andi looked down and concealed the bracelet in her hands. "No. It's nothing. It's, umm—it's—" She looked around the room.

"Andi?" Jenny didn't let her go. "Why do you have Mickey's charm bracelet?"

"It's just a bracelet. I didn't think anyone would care. But when her parents got here, well, I was thinking I should give it to them. But I didn't want them to know."

"Know what?" Jenny asked. "Andi, did you have something to do with Mickey's death?"

"I don't know!" Andi cried. "I don't know. I went to talk to her early on Tuesday. It was the only time I had open. You know how busy things got this week. No one else was in the room. I shook her to wake her up, and she fell off the bed. I just wanted to talk to her. I took the bracelet. That's all. I didn't want to hurt her."

"Why didn't you call the police?" Jenny grabbed Andi's hands and squeezed them, trying to calm her down. "Or tell me or anyone?"

Andi was sobbing now and Jenny could hear footsteps outside. She tried to calm her down, to quiet her at least until she got the whole story.

"I didn't want them to think I killed her. I just wanted to talk." Andi had buried herself in her arms and plunged backward into the corner as far as she would go.

"What were you going to talk to Mickey about?"

Andi's sobs shook her whole body. Jenny couldn't do anything. She pressed her hands flat against the bed and waited. Finally, Andi took a breath and tried to push her words out. "Why she left me. Why she was my friend while I was helping her, and then she left me. And then she died and it's because of me and I didn't mean it. I didn't want her to get hurt."

"What do you mean? What happened?" Jenny's brow furrowed so hard it hurt.

Andi pulled her knees up, burying her face in her hands and tucking her head low into her lap. "I gave away the door code."

Jenny's patting slowed. "The door code? For the rental?"

Andi's head bobbed. "Yes. I asked Hugo to bring the extra supplies. But I wrote the code down for him, and he lost it. I'm the one who gave the code away and the killer must have found it. If it wasn't for me, Mickey wouldn't be dead."

"Oh, Andi." Jenny didn't know what to say. "We don't know what happened. How would someone even know what it went to? And even if you handed it directly to the killer you didn't give it with that intent. You were delivering supplies, so by that reasoning it's my fault."

"No. I didn't mean that. I'm so sorry." Andi's

sobs had lessened, but her face was still crumpled and red.

"Stop that." Jenny took a breath and tried to be responsible. "We still don't know. We're figuring out a little more every day, and knowing things like this will help. Have you told the police?"

Andi shook her head.

"Why don't you start there?" Jenny said.

Andi nodded.

"Why didn't you tell the police the first day? And why did you take her bracelet?"

Andi looked at it sitting in her open palm. "I really didn't think anyone would miss it. I just wanted to remember her."

The door banged open, and Helen dragged several bags through it. "Oh. I didn't know you were in here. But guess what just happened. You'll never guess. I got my luggage back and look!" Helen's voice rose in pitch every few syllables. When she finally stopped she looked at Andi's tear-stained face and hesitated. "Am I interrupting?"

"No, of course not." Jenny turned back to Andi, the bracelet hanging limply from her fingers. "You should return that to the Stevens before they go."

Andi nodded.

"And call the police," Jenny told her.

She nodded again and skirted Helen, her face abashed.

Helen's smile faltered as she watched the girl leave. "I was definitely interrupting something."

She dropped her bags and pulled one on top of the others. "That's weird."

"Yeah," Jenny agreed, but otherwise ignored the unspoken question. "Tell me what happened."

"The police sent my stuff back. I even have my grandma's quilt! I was so worried." Helen unzipped the bag and started pulling things out of it.

"It's not evidence?" It wasn't that Jenny wanted her to be without it, but she hadn't thought they'd give it up before the case was solved.

Then Helen pulled the quilt out of the bag, and Jenny's stomach dropped.

"That's your grandma's quilt?" It was beautiful, with red and white trim pieces and red embroidery over large sections of white fabric. "That can't be right. I thought your grandma's was red and white stars. It's a quilted redwork."

Helen raised an eyebrow and spread out her quilt. "No. I'm pretty sure this is it. It's the one I packed up. Look, she stitched her name right in this corner."

"I'm sorry. I'm just confused. I'm super happy for you though."

But if that was Helen's, whose was the blanket Mickey was wrapped in? And where had it come from?

"The Stevenses are leaving. Do you want to go say goodbye?" Cherry asked, leaning into the room behind her.

"Of course." Jenny excused herself and walked with Cherry down the hall.

A Body in Redwork

"Where's Andi going?" Cherry sounded nervous but she smiled brightly as they walked. "She's not going to keep messing with the decorations, is she?"

Jenny took Cherry's hand. "I just had a conversation with Andi. She's not trying to take over. She's been struggling with Mickey's death. They knew each other before, and this has been really hard for her."

Cherry stopped walking, "Oh my goodness. That's terrible. What do you think I should do?"

Andi appeared at the end of the hallway.

"I don't know. I'm sure you'll figure it out. I just wanted to let you know."

Cherry nodded not listening anymore as Andi started to leave. She took several quick steps down the hallway and called out to the other assistant. 'Andi, I was hoping you could help me with something. I don't know how to replace all the broken plants. I thought you might have an idea."

Jenny stared open-mouthed as Cherry's kind gesture pulled Andi from her introverted state. Together they began discussing plans and Jenny shook her head. "Sometimes it's really that simple."

Helen spoke up from beside her. "It's amazing what jealousy can tear apart and what a simple phrase can repair."

Jenny looked after them. It was Friday morning. Almost the last day of the retreat. There was no reason to fix the decorations. Andi had red eyes and Cherry was talking too quickly but they were making plans. Some things weren't about the logic. Sometimes you had to heal the heart.

Heal the heart. Jenny backed up down the hallway and slipped into the storage room. She pulled her design board down. It was a dismal array of clues. Jenny knew of several people in this game who needed to heal. Jenny grabbed a fence rail block and labeled it Maggie. She put it on the board directly beneath Mickey's block and did a quick scan. She'd talked to everyone on there except for Maggie.

Jenny looked at her phone Friday morning. If people were going to start going home tonight she was running out of time, and Jenny had one more interrogation to make.

13

Jenny took the grand staircase down to the main level of the Sewing Center. At the bottom of the steps the main floor practically writhed with activity. People were everywhere. The noise level had risen by several decibels since the convention hall had opened to the public.

Sally and Owen stood at the back of their booth with a girl Jenny didn't recognize.

Jenny caught Sally's eye and rushed her companions into the booth. Then opened her arms to Jenny.

Jenny stiffened as Sally hugged her and she pulled back. "Is everything alright?"

The movement of the guests and quilters had Jenny on edge, so different than the effect the crowds usually had on her. It didn't help that she still had the nagging feeling that something was off with the Harper Wovens team, and she wondered if the very woman she was talking to could be a murderer.

nny shoved her hands in her pockets. "I'm
Has Officer Wilkins been by? I wondered if he
ny new information."

ally wrapped her arms together, one hand going
ne base of her neck. "No. I haven't heard
hing. Have you? It's only been a couple days.
uld I be more worried?"

"No, I'm sure it's fine." Jenny knew full well the
officer had new information. She just didn't know
if he believed her or when he'd follow up on things.
"Who's helping you? I half expected to get a call to
be here."

Sally glanced at the booth. "Well, she's, umm,
one of our basics designers. She lives in the area.
We just needed someone to be here with us since,
you know . . . I'm sorry we won't be working
together after all. Owen told me what he said to you.
I think the idea that you had anything to do with the
death of Mickey and Liz is crazy, but I can't change
his mind."

Jenny put a hand up, cutting Sally off. "It's fine.
You don't have any extra Harper Wovens designer
pins, do you?"

"Oh? Did you want one? I have a couple,
somewhere. I actually don't know where they are."
She laughed nervously, her hands in her pockets
while she made a show of looking around. "We had
several with us, I think. I'm not supposed to give
them out, but I might be able to snag one for you."

"I don't need one." She wanted one, but she
didn't need it. The pin probably wouldn't make her

feel any different, anyhow.

The nervous woman in front of her searching boxes and pockets didn't feel like a killer. Of course, she wasn't acting frantic and defensive about Owen or her business right now.

"Sally? Can I ask you a personal question?"

Sally stopped turning circles and came back. "Are you still thinking about Mickey?"

"And Lizzy." The wall of rainbow-colored fabric billowed beside them, the mass of people on the other side causing the fabric to undulate delicately. "Did Owen and Mickey ever have a relationship?"

Sally took a step back, the pinch of her brows giving away her displeasure. She gave a jerky shake of the head. "No. Not really. I mean, they may have shown interest in each other once, but after I hired her . . . No, Mickey knew Owen and I were destined to be together. She wouldn't do that to me."

Jenny nodded. *Old girlfriends disappearing. It's what you wanted, right?* Jenny took another breath. There was more she needed to know. "And what about Lizzy? Did she and Owen?"

Sally gasped. "Jenny, why? No. No, Lizzy wouldn't. I wouldn't—I mean, she was so busy. No."

Jenny kept nodding. Sally's denial felt forced. The truth hovered just at the tip of her tongue.

Hugh stepped out of the back of the booth. "Sally, you're needed when you have a moment."

He disappeared into the booth, and Jenny turned

to Sally in confusion. "Doesn't he have his own booth?"

"Yes." Sally shrugged. "But he came to help anyway. I try to ignore him most of the time. He's very helpful, but if I give him too much attention, he acts like he owns the place. I think he wants to be my best friend or something. I'm not sure he knows how close Owen and I are."

Jenny didn't get a chance to respond before Owen leaned his head out. His eyes fell on Jenny and narrowed. "You're not supposed to be here." He redirected his focus to Sally. "There's a police officer here and he's scaring the guests. Are you done talking?"

"I'm coming." Sally turned to Owen like a lifeline. "Have either of you seen any more notes?" Jenny asked. "You know, the little red notecards?"

Sally shook her head. "No. I can let you know if I find one."

"That's fine. I'll talk to you later."

Sally passed Owen, and he looked back at Jenny.

"You need to go. Unless you have a police badge, our issues are none of your business. I don't want to see you back here."

Jenny shook her head, frustrated he was being so uncooperative. After a moment of glaring at her, Owen disappeared back into the booth.

Jenny took a moment to clear her mind. She hadn't learned anything. Except that Sally would deny anything when it came to Owen being with anyone but her. And that her pins were missing.

A Body in Redwork

She wished she could search the booth again, but Maggie was only one booth away and she was more important than pins.

The jungle-themed Pears & Gin booth had survived the collapse of the wall that had fallen on Jenny. She couldn't tell whether they'd had to rebuild or if the damage had been entirely on the Harper Wovens side, but the vines grew up the walls and fabric flowers the size of kiddie pools clung to the wall as if they'd always meant to be there.

Jenny slid between the booths to keep from distracting them while she looked for Maggie. People filled the little cubicle at the front of the display, admiring the color and creativity. Ruby Carter was handing out samples to everyone that passed while Maggie smiled and pointed at various display items. Jenny stepped forward.

"Maggie, it's Jenny. I don't know if you remember me, but I have a question for you."

Maggie's bright smile faltered slightly, but she stepped to the side of the booth with Jenny.

"What can I do for you?"

"Are you still seeing Owen Teak?" Jenny caught the flinch on Maggie's face and bit her lip, wishing she hadn't been so blunt.

"That unfortunately has nothing to do with our fabric. Is there something else I can help you with? Things are pretty busy, and I—"

"I know it's none of my business. But as you know, Sally and Owen have been targeted with the recent deaths of their designers. Have you noticed anything strange around them in the past few days?"

"We're not dating. So no, I haven't noticed anything." Maggie turned on her heel, and Jenny followed her to the back of the booth.

"That surprises me because I heard—"

"It doesn't really matter what you heard. We haven't been dating for a while." Maggie looked upset but she stopped trying to escape. "Sally made sure of that."

"What did Sally do?" Jenny shifted, suddenly feeling like they were speaking with bullhorns and wanting to stay as far from the Harper Wovens booth as possible.

Maggie hesitated. She released a breath. "Sally did everything she could to break us up. She canceled plans, called Owen into work during his days off because she *needed* him. I applied to work with them. And let me be clear, I applied because I liked the company, not to be closer to Owen. But I should have known better. Sally belittled my work and told me she'd never work with me. Owen, and everyone else on the team, said they'd love to work with me. Sally blackballed me."

"That must have made you pretty angry." Jenny tried to gauge her response. Maggie didn't hold the same fierceness as Sally when it came to Owen, but after the conversation at the Meet and Greet and hearing her now, it felt like bitterness. Sally had hurt her.

"I mean, yeah. She's basically trapped Owen with the business. He can't do anything she doesn't want without upsetting their partnership." Maggie glanced back at the owner, Ruby, showing off fabric kits to a potential customer. Maggie gestured for Jenny to follow her. "Come this way."

They passed a large section of trailing vines in a hot pink floral print and a four-foot jungle bloom hanging over a section of quilt patterns.

Jenny paused. One of them looked familiar.

When Maggie realized Jenny had stopped moving, she turned around and leaned back in the booth, whispering. "Can we go out back? I don't care if Sally hears what I say. I just don't want Ruby to look bad if anyone hears me complaining."

"Have you ever made this pattern in red before?" Jenny asked. It was a simple pattern, but a pretty one. A star quilt, offset by four patch blocks.

"Of course. I think we have one right over—" Maggie stopped for a moment. She looked under a table and then moved out the back of the booth, looking in several places. "You know, I could have sworn we had several at the beginning of the week, but I can't find them now." Maggie kept looking and Jenny followed her to the back of the booth.

"How does something like that go missing without being noticed?" Jenny asked.

Maggie laughed. "Have you noticed how much stuff we have in there? I was just excited the booth was more spacious than we expected. We still didn't fit it all in. Oh! You know what, I let Lizzy Rose borrow them. I was supposed to get her patterns to go with them. Some kind of collaboration. Hugo picked them up for her on Monday."

Jenny nodded, backing up toward the stairs. "Thanks, Maggie, that was really helpful. I've . . . got to go now."

She paused, looking at the Harper Wovens booth. That would be the easiest way to find an answer, but Owen didn't want her there. When Hugo came out the back, Jenny started up the stairs as quickly as her body would carry her. She looked back once to see Hugo watching her. Jenny didn't wait to see what he would say. She had bigger things on her mind.

Jenny flew down the hallway, stopping at Helen's door. No one was inside, but Helen's grandmother's quilt sat folded and taunting at the end of her bed. The quilt she'd thought Mickey had been wrapped in. She let the door slam shut and moved to the next room, closing it when no one was there and moving on. Tilly sat on the couch in the gathering room, and Bernie and Dotty worked on two different projects in the corner booth with the Hugo Hensen label on the patterns.

"Has anyone seen Helen?" Jenny asked, and got a room full of blank stares. She took a breath and tried to slow down. "I have a Lizzy Rose question. Has anyone seen her?"

Tilly shook her head. "I haven't seen Lizzy since the morning we found Mickey."

Bernie didn't look up, and Dotty jumped when she spoke. "And the night before. She came to visit with Helen."

206

"And yell at Mickey," Maura reminded them.

Jenny bit her lip. "I remember that. I'm actually looking for Helen. Lizzy borrowed some quilts, and I'm trying to find out who they were for. I thought Helen might know."

Maura shook her head and leaned over Bernie's project to examine the stitching.

"Let me know if she comes back." Jenny moved back into the hallway.

Frustration at not being able to connect the dots ate at her. She wanted to growl or hide or run screaming down the hall, but none of those things would take care of the mess that had been left around them. Jenny made her way to the storage room without screaming or growling once. She was slightly proud of that fact.

In the quiet room, she let out a breath. This was just a quilt, she told herself. With pieces that fit together into a pattern that would make sense, if she could only be sure she had them all.

Jenny opened her design board. There were definitely pieces missing. She touched the blue fence rail block she'd labeled "Maggie". She wouldn't take it off. She was jealous and bitter and that was a dangerous combination. But could she kill someone?

Mickey was surrounded by quilt blocks now. Lizzy's churn dash, Sally's hourglass, and Helen's nine patch. Maggie's fence rail supported the bottom. She reached up and removed Lizzy and Helen's blocks. She was almost disappointed to do so. While she was certain it wasn't them, it left so few options. Sally, and Maggie were the shining beacons left on the board.

Jenny picked up Maggie's block and moved it to sit beside Mickey's block. The sashing labeled "fight with Mickey" was still there. Jenny looked at it. The fight, while it had been upsetting, had nothing to do with Mickey's death. Jenny pulled it off, thinking about the clues that were left. The notecards were the biggest clue, and she hadn't even put them on the board. She pulled out another sashing, labeled it "notecards" and stuck it right next to Maggie. She had painted the cards and someone had written in them. She grabbed another sashing and wrote "Quilt patterns" on it. She laid it on the board above Maggie's block. Maggie had loaned the finished quilts to Lizzy, but Lizzy had gotten them for someone else. Who?

Lizzy. The board felt empty without her, and Jenny realized it was because this wasn't just Mickey's murder. Mickey and Lizzy both held clues to the murder, and Jenny needed to be looking at them both.

Jenny moved Maggie's block and put Lizzy back on the board next to Mickey. She added a block labeled "sisters" and one with "amaryllis plant" on it. The stolen line and the notecards applied to both. Maybe she should put Sally's other scarf on the board. Sally wasn't in custody, but she'd had evidence at both crime scenes and motive and opportunity to kill both designers, even if one of them was her sister.

The door code was another one. Andi had given the door code to Hugo. Had he given Sally the code?

A floor board creaked, and Jenny looked at the door. No one was there, but the hairs on the back of her neck pricked at all of the pieces coming together.

The killer had used Maggie's cards, with or without her help. Jenny didn't know. And Jenny hadn't been threatened until after she'd discovered Owen and Maggie at the Meet and Greet, where she learned that Lizzy's pin was replaced after she died.

The designers pin. She labeled a cornerstone with the name and stuck it on the board. She set it by Lizzy and then Maggie finally plugging it in the only corner that would touch both the victims and Sally. She held the pins.

The cornerstone was only two and a half inches, but it felt heavy.

There were only a few pieces that were consistent from murder to murder. The quilts the girls had been wrapped in, the note card poems, and the pins.

The pins. The girls who'd been killed were already Harper Wovens designers, and still the killer had gone to the trouble of placing new pins on each of their chests. Like they wanted to be sure the girls were identified. And now the few pins Sally had were missing. If Jenny could find out who took the pins, maybe she could find out who the killer was.

Jenny closed her design board. It felt like she was working out a new pattern. She just kept trying the pieces out in different ways, hoping something would click.

A knock at the door pulled Jenny out of her reverie, and Helen leaned in.

"Hey, the girls said you were looking for me."

"Yes." Jenny jumped out of her seat. "Did Lizzy ever say anything about borrowing some two-toned quilts from the booth next to theirs? Red and white and green and white, things like that? Maggie seemed to think they were collaborating on something."

Helen pursed her lips and shook her head. "Not that I know of. Why? Is it important?"

"Maybe. I'm trying to figure out whose quilt Mickey was wrapped in, and I think it came from the Pears & Gin booth. But Lizzy took the quilts for someone, and I don't know who."

"Have you asked Sally?"

Jenny glanced at the closed board. "No. Owen isn't letting me alone with her. He thinks I had something to do with Mickey's and Lizzy's deaths because I was there when both were found."

Helen's brow furrowed, and Jenny slipped through the door.

"It's all right." She tried to make herself feel better. "Someone else knows who they're for."

Helen fell into step behind Jenny as they walked back toward the corner gathering room. "I think I saw some quilts like that at her rental when I first

210

got here. There was a blue one too."

Jenny stopped and turned to her. "You where she was staying?"

"Yeah," Helen said. "We traded codes wl first got to town. We planned to work or things together, all three of us."

"All three? Oh, you, Helen, and —"

"Mickey. All three of us." Helen's voi heavy on her friends name.

"You don't happen to remember that code, do you?"

Helen nodded, "Yeah, but she was staying will Sally and Owen."

14

It took a little convincing, including the promise that no one would know Helen had given Jenny the code, but now she stood outside the rental cottage behind the Sewing Center where Lizzy had been staying with Sally and Owen. It was a two-story place within walking distance of the events. The Harper Wovens crew was staying in the upstairs portion of the building.

Jenny climbed the steps and put in the code. The door swung open, and she stepped into an updated flat. The couch wasn't brand new but in good shape, the whole room a blend of cream and navy with a yellow and persimmon color splashed on the accents. The counters were clear of anything but a few fast food packages, and the only blankets Jenny could see were the throw blankets decoratively stashed in a basket by the television console. Not a quilt in sight.

It wasn't a promising start. She scanned the room and moved to the next door. Two beds under cream-colored coverlets were set on either side of the room. A stack of luggage was piled neatly in the corner, and on top of the far bed was Lizzy Rose's black and gray coat and scarf that she'd worn the first day of the retreat.

Jenny did a quick scan even opening a few empty drawers. No quilts, no pins, no stash of scarves labeled murder weapons.

Jenny's breathing quickened. What was she even looking for? If there was no stack of quilts matching the ones at the murder scenes, would Jenny even know what to look for?

She opened the next door and found another bedroom. This one wasn't quite as clean. The navy bedspread was pulled back, and Jenny had to step over a discarded pair of clothes before she made it fully into the room. Still, other than a lack of organization, it looked like Owen was as clear of murder as anyone else. Unfortunately, this didn't surprise her.

The next door was locked. Jenny jiggled the door handle and scanned the room again but didn't see any way to get in. She dropped her bag on the floor and looked under the door. Nothing. Jenny sat by the door for a moment, wondering if she'd be able to get through, when a sound startled her. A car had pulled into the drive, and she was instantly on her feet. Even without anything to show for it, she couldn't break her promise to Helen. She wouldn't let anyone know she was there.

She checked the window, grateful she'd walked

the short block instead of driving herself. In the driveway sat a sleek blue sedan. A car door opened, and Jenny pulled back. She would have to hide. With as busy as things were, nobody would stay for long. She just needed to hide for a minute. She swung past the locked door, knocking a picture off the wall as she tried to get into Lizzy's room.

Jenny picked up the picture to hang it back on the wall, and a key tumbled to the ground. Voices from outside came in through the window, and Jenny didn't hesitate. She slapped the picture onto the wall and shoved the key into the lock of the last door. It slid in and turned seamlessly. Jenny opened the door, but instead of the third bedroom she'd expected to find, Jenny found herself in a stairwell.

She turned, locking the door behind her and took the steps down. Pausing halfway between the door she'd just left and the one at the bottom of the hall. Trapped between two doors Jenny suddenly remembered her bag on the floor upstairs.

"Oh no." She breathed the words and hurried up the stairs. A door swung open, and Jenny froze. Footsteps walked through the building but they weren't where Jenny expected. Someone was walking around in the ground floor apartment.

Jenny opened the upper door and leaned around it, She grabbed her bag from the floor and closed herself in the stairwell again. A drawer slammed nearby, and someone muttered something.

"In the drawer it's supposed to be in the drawer."

Jenny recognized Maggie's muffled voice this

time. Jenny took the steps down to the lower level as quietly as she could, trying to get closer to the doorframe. Maggie shuffled around some more. "There it is, ouch, stupid pin. This is ridiculous."

The pin. Jenny tried to place the sounds as Maggie moved through the room. Was Maggie staying in the basement? Maggie was the one who had arranged the quilts. She'd done the notecards. Jenny wasn't sure what her connection was to Mickey unless Mickey and Owen really had been in a relationship at some point, despite Sally's denial.

Maggie had been there before Jenny was attacked and based on the conversation she'd had with Owen she had every reason to want his "Old girlfriends" dead. She was helping him escape.

Maggie's voice grew softer as she sang, "Jingle bells, quilters smell." The door shut behind her. Jenny wanted to rush after her and stop her right then.

She tried the key in the lower door praying it would be another matching lock. It didn't work. Jenny shook the door handle. No. She shook it again, slamming her hand against the door. "No!"

She was so close to proof and she couldn't get through the door.

Jenny climbed the stairs. Her knees were starting to ache after her third time up, but she pushed herself and grabbed the door handle. She made sure to leave the door locked for when Sally and Owen came back. As she passed the counter, a flash of red stopped Jenny in her tracks. Jenny pulled a red paper from under the cup carrier. The paper came out and Jenny let out a breath of relief. It was a candy wrapper. Dropping the wrapper back on the counter, Jenny checked to make sure the driveway was clear before she left the upstairs apartment. She locked the door behind her, hurried down the steps and crossed the street to the sidewalk that would lead her to the Sewing Center.

Jenny pulled out her phone and dialed the police station.

"Hamilton police department. How can I help you?" a sweet voice on the other end of the line greeted her.

"I need to talk to Officer Wilkins. I have information regarding the recent murders." Jenny had reached the back corner of the Sewing Center when he picked up.

"What can I do for you?" Officer Wilkins said on the other end of the line.

"Officer Wilkins. This is Jenny Doan. I found out something you should know. Maggie is a designer at Pears & Gin fabrics. She's the one who paints the cards that have been left at the murders. I don't know if she's leaving another or if it's already done but she just went to her apartment to pick up one of the pins that she leaves on the bodies when she dresses them."

"Maggie? We've talked to her, and I don't think she's a problem." Officer Wilkins sounded skeptical, even distant.

"Did you ask her about her relationship with Owen?" Jenny looked around the street, anxious to be saying such sensitive things where anyone could hear. "Did you ask Owen about his relationship with the previous victims? Maggie's got to have the quilts or the pins or extra cards. Just go check, please?"

"Jenny. I don't think it's as simple as that, but I'll see what I can do."

Jenny sighed. "Thank you." Now she just had to go watch Harper Wovens and try to figure out Maggie's game plan.

Men and women spilled from around the corner of the building, and Jenny moved forward to meet them. Confusion created a communal voice that Jenny couldn't understand. . A flash of turquoise florals on a bright yellow blouse identified Cherry moving through the crowd.

Jenny called out to her, but she didn't hear. Cherry stopped by the door talking to Tilly, but as Jenny pushed her way through, Cherry disappeared inside the building.

"What's going on?" Jenny asked when she made it to Tilly.

"Jenny!" Tilly looked at her in surprise. "Cherry's looking for you."

Jenny glanced back to the building. "Is everything okay?"

"It looks bad, doesn't it." Tilly rolled her eyes. "Just mob mentality. There was a power outage, and the maintenance guys, or whoever is in charge, couldn't fix it. With it getting dark soon, they shut things down early. Everyone had to leave."

"It looked like a fire was happening." Jenny

couldn't believe the chaos and the amount of pe———
leaving. Everyone stood huddled in groups, watchi.
the building as if it might light back up. "Has anyone
seen Maggie? From Pears & Gin? Or Sally?"

Tilly shook her head, only half listening.

Maura came up behind Tilly. "Is it going to be a
problem for us to stay here tonight?"

Jenny raised her eyebrows. "Shoot." She looked
up at the sky. It wasn't snowing, but it was cold. The
street lights lit up the sidewalk and all the women in
their winter coats. "I don't know. If the power's out,
there won't be any heat. We might be better off
packing into the local's homes, at least for the night.
Where are all the designers?" She looked around but
didn't see the faces of any of the designers she
hoped to find.

"They took the designers out the back. So they
could get a few things after the crowd left." Maura
was still watching the sky. "Can we at least go in
and get our things?"

Jenny looked around but couldn't see Andi or
anyone on the event team. She turned back to Tilly
and Maura. "Let's go together. I'll find Cherry and
you get your stuff."

The girls nodded and Jenny tried not to be too
noticeable as they slipped into the building while
everyone else was leaving.

The building's quiet was a stark change from the
noise outside. Footsteps echoed, the dimming light
making the lack of ambient noise more noticeable.
Eerie shadows changed the setting from inviting to

erving as the sun fell from the sky already
arkened by the clouds and weather.

At the top of the steps, the women split up, each
going to collect their things. Jenny opened the door
to the gathering room, hoping to see Cherry waiting
there. But in the dimming light, all she could see
were the shapes of furniture scattered around the
room. Jenny's quilt lay in pieces on her table. She'd
worked on it here and there over the week, but it
wasn't done. Since she'd be filming the next day,
she crossed the dark room and gathered the pieces
of her un-quilted lemoyne star. She'd hoped to show
the new version of the quilt on the tutorial, but the
chances of finishing it were getting slimmer all the
time. She grabbed it and turned to leave. In the
darkness, she knocked over several things from
another table.

"Shoot." The ground was even darker than the
tables, and Jenny had to turn on her phone's
flashlight to be able to see.

Bernie and Dotty's hand work lay on the ground
along with the patterns. Jenny picked up the pieces
and placed them on the table. Bernie's was almost
done, and Jenny moved her thumb over a five-
pointed lily in the corner. Jenny had seen the pattern
before, but it took her a moment to place it.

Then she knew. She looked at the other pattern.
Dotty's was almost done, but Jenny could see the
signature lily taking shape in the center of her piece.

The shape played with her mind and Jenny
opened up the pictures of the notecards she'd been

flipping through for days. There in the very first poem. Jenny had taken a picture of it while it had been sitting on the quilt and behind the corner of the notecard was a perfect little five pointed lily. Bernie and Dotty were stitching the signature that she'd seen on the corner of the murder quilts. Jenny sat down and stared at the image. She didn't have a picture of the green quilt but she knew she'd seen it.

People moved in the hallway, and Jenny stood, hurrying to help them. Tilly and Maura both had an armful of things. They had bumped into each other in the dark and were scrambling to hold onto their belongings.

Jenny's heart felt like it was beating out of her chest. She forced herself to relax, trying to look at ease. "Go on down. I'm still looking for Cherry."

They didn't even think twice. They went down the stairs. Jenny only looked over her shoulder briefly before moving back into the building.

"Cherry?" Jenny thought she was grateful for an excuse to go snooping around, but as she moved away from the big windows at the front of the building, everything got darker very quickly. Something fell in the convention area below, and Jenny called out again. "Cherry?"

If Cherry got caught up in the next scheme, Jenny would never forgive herself. Someone muttered, and Jenny hurried down the steps. The building suddenly felt huge. Cherry could be anywhere in it.

She relaxed when she didn't see anyone. No one

was there. Maybe it really was a power outage. Light from the front windows spilled over the booths, and all Jenny could see was silhouettes of fabric and metal. Jenny stepped off the staircase, ready to exit the building, when she saw the quilt folded up next to the backside of the Harper Wovens booth.

It was darker on the ground with all the booth curtains blocking the light. Jenny turned her flashlight on. The quilt was blue like Maggie had said, and the pattern matched the ones that had been used previously. Jenny turned over the corner of the quilt, and there it was. The five-pointed lily.

Jenny looked up. The killer had to be nearby. As she moved her flashlight, the beam caught a slip of red paper crumbled on the table.

Jenny picked it up. The card had been torn in half, crumpled, and the cover discarded. It didn't hide the words.

Silent night, final night.
Your death will bring a shameful light.
The lies you tell, you tell to yourself.
You chose who thrives and who stays on the shelf.
Admit this truth or you'll see
It's the last chance you'll have to choose me.

The last chance you'll have to choose me. Jenny looked up. She knew exactly who she was looking

222

for, but it wasn't who she'd thought when she walked in the building.

Jenny pulled back the curtain. At first glance the booth looked empty, and then she saw him.

"Hugo?" Jenny asked, moving toward the couch in the center of the booth.

But the face Jenny saw wasn't Hugo's at all. Jenny flashed her light up. Sally Harper lay back across the couch, painted like a doll, a giant sleeping dolly.

"Oh my gosh." Jenny dropped her phone and grabbed Sally's shoulder.

A noise sounded behind her, and Jenny spun around, facing the Pears & Gin booth. A figure appeared, and Jenny gripped the edge of the couch.

"Don't do that," Maggie said as she moved slowly closer. "We just got her painted so nicely."

"We?" Jenny turned to look around.

Something hit her head, and everything went black.

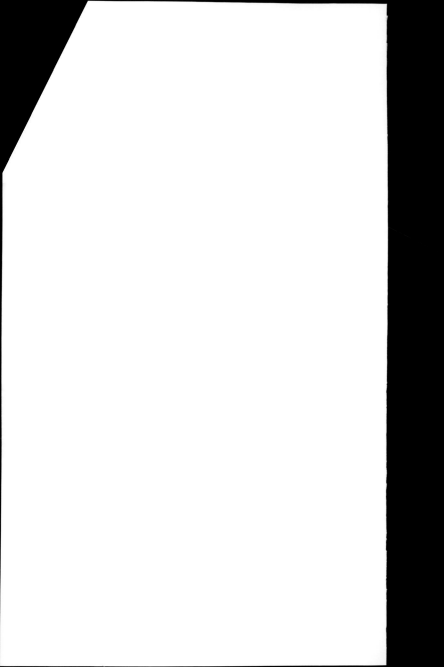

15

"Make sure it's tight enough."

Jenny lay very still as she came back to consciousness. Through slitted eyes, she saw Hugo hover over Sally, giving her set up the final touches.

"She has a gift for getting in the way," Hugo said. "And I don't need her causing problems."

"I'm not incompetent." Maggie twisted a fabric strip tightly around Jenny's wrist. She had tied her to the pole between the Harper Wovens booth and the Pears & Gin booth. It was the same area that had collapsed before.

"No, you're not incompetent. Just impatient. We would have had more time to take care of Sally if we'd waited until everyone had gone home."

"If we waited until everyone had gone home, we would have no alibi," Maggie shot back. "This chaos out there is perfect. It doesn't take long to paint a woman up."

"She's right," Jenny's groggy voice drew the attention of Hugo along with a frustrated tug on her wrist from Maggie.

"Of course I'm right." Maggie walked away, disappearing behind the booth.

Jenny leaned back on the metal pole. It swayed but not enough to give way. "This is the perfect time to kill someone," she said. "And I'm so glad you chose Sally. She lied about everything."

Hugo glanced back. His paintbrush paused and then dipped into a deep orange paint. He went back to touch up her lips again.

"I know. She told me so many times that we'd start something together. That we would be a team. Do you know how many times I got to design with her?" He looked at Jenny, then back at Sally before answering. "None. Not once would she lower herself to create with me."

He pulled back and grabbed a rag, wiping his brush in the cloth.

"I wasn't asking for much. I'm a good designer. I just wanted to be on her team. The others weren't worthy of her. Sally's fabric was genius, and when she stopped, I knew I could be the one that would make her create again." He looked down and swept a piece of her hair back. "We could have been great."

Jenny couldn't help thinking about Cherry and Andi, and how they'd fought all week trying to outdo the other person. But in the end, they'd been able to have compassion and work together. Hugo had taken his personal competition so much further, literally taking out the competition.

Maggie reappeared and made gagging noises.

"Please. She had to go. The woman was crazy. Now you can design anything you think she would like. Name them all after her, for all I care. I'm just glad to get her away from Owen. The man didn't understand the value of a good restraining order."

She braided Sally's hair to the side and held up a little red card, examining it before setting her hair across her shoulder. Then Maggie turned back to Jenny. "You weren't supposed to be here. We told you not to be here."

Jenny looked around. "Is Owen a part of this?"

Maggie scoffed. "Owen? No. He didn't have a clue what he was doing, but we warned you. Or did you not notice the message we sent to your room?"

Hugo stood in front of her now. He crossed his arms and tipped his head as if examining her in the darkness. "If you'd listened to any of these warnings we wouldn't be having this conversation right now. You wouldn't have to die."

Maggie turned. "You want to kill her too? We haven't even killed Sally yet."

"We can't kill her yet. You know that." Hugo dug through a bag and came out with a pair of gloves. "I want Sally to know what she gave up by not choosing me. I want her to see the consequences of her choices. Having Jenny here makes it even more perfect."

With his gloved hands, Hugo pulled out a long floral scarf that Jenny had seen Sally wearing the day before.

"How did you get all those?" Jenny asked, not

ven worrying if she upset him.

Hugo glared, and Jenny's phone rang from where she'd dropped it before. Hugo ignored it. "It's time to go, Jenny."

No. It wasn't. She needed to delay him. Jenny leaned back, feeling the pole sway like before. She was still on the ground but she twisted her wrists, gripping the lower part of the pole, and shoved back. The leg shifted making a loud scraping on the ground.

"Be careful." Maggie yelled from where she was dressing Sally.

"What are you going to do with me?" Jenny couldn't do much, but if getting Hugo talking would save her life, Jenny could talk.

"Do you want to see?" He knelt in front of her.

Jenny sucked in a breath. Despite telling herself to act normal, Hugo's face so close to hers it muddled her mind. Her heart raced, and Jenny couldn't imagine how she'd get away from this man. She pushed back again.

"What are you doing?" He looked behind her. Her wrists were still tied and Jenny shook her head.

"Sorry." She muttered, "I'm claustrophobic, you were too close."

Hugo's lip pulled up in a sneer. "I'm going to make you a twin dolly to Sally. Paint you both to match. What do you think? Won't that be such fun for the holidays?"

Maggie looked Jenny up and down. "They're not twins."

228

"No. But paint can work miracles." Hugo stretched the scarf out, and the phone rang again.

"Do you think someone's tracking me?" Jenny wiggled to the side, and Hugo looked back, his eyes tracking where the phone lit up against the wall.

He stood, tromped over to the phone, and picked it up. "You think they're tracking this thing?" He threw it at the corner of the booth, hitting a cluster of metal poles and destroying it before her eyes.

"Jenny?" Cherry's voice came, and Hugo looked back, distracted by the second voice that shouldn't be there.

"I'm here," she called.

Hugo turned back just as Jenny stood up.

She gripped the pole and yanked it to the side. The chandelier dropped several feet, almost landing on Sally, but like before it caught suspended over the couch. Maggie disappeared, her footsteps pounding up the stairs as the metal poles tumbled over Hugo. One of them hit him from behind and he dropped to the ground.

Cherry rushed into view.

"Let me help you." Cherry was instantly by her side, but Jenny shook her off.

"No, call the police. And go get Maggie. She's gone upstairs." Jenny slid her bonds along the pole until she reached the top. She slipped her fabric handcuffs over the edge of the pole and waved Cherry on. "Go, hurry."

Cherry's lip quivered slightly, but she ran to the

ack of the building, her feet pounding up the stairs as she chased after the other culprit.

In the mess of poles and broken booth features, Jenny tried to push Sally's couch back. A groan confirmed Maggie's story that Sally wasn't dead yet, and Jenny shoved harder, trying to get it to a safe place.

A sharp piece of metal protruded from the largest of the poles. Jenny rubbed the fabric of her wrists against it. "Sally," Jenny hissed as threads snapped and the fabric came slowly apart. "Sally, are you awake?"

There was no response.

Jenny's bands gave a final pop, and Jenny let out a gasp of relief. She was going to be free.

One of the poles behind her clanked to the floor, and a groan from Hugo kickstarted Jenny's adrenaline.

"Don't be awake," she said softly, moving away from the mess of poles where Hugo had fallen.

Jenny put Sally on the settee and pushed her into the corner. She grabbed a stray swatch of fabric and wiped at the painted lashes around Sally's eyes. "Sally, you need to wake up."

Jenny rubbed harshly at Sally's cheeks, only garnering a whisper of a groan. "Come on, Sally." She lifted her, and Sally's head lolled to the side. Jenny slid an arm under her shoulder.

Jenny stumbled through the jungle gym of broken framework and pulled Sally with her. Finally making it to the back of the booth, Jenny

stepped through the fabric panels of the back wa
as a low growl came from the other side.

"Shoot," Jenny breathed, and walked Sally faster
out through the back door. She stopped. She didn't
want to lose Hugo, but there was no way she was
going back in there with a man who'd just confessed
his plans to kill her. Movement from inside
tightened the pain in her chest. She couldn't even
call the police to redirect them here.

She set Sally down against the porch railing and
cracked the door open.

It was quiet inside. The growl she'd heard was
gone. Maybe she'd imagined it. The metal poles that
had fallen on him were pretty heavy duty.

Sirens wailed, and Jenny cracked the door a little
further. Something crashed and somewhere inside
Cherry screamed. Jenny's heart panicked. She tried
to track the sound but there was nothing. It was quiet
and dark.

A scuffling of sound and voices came from the
stairway. That wasn't very far. If Jenny could keep
calm she could make it to the stairs.

Sally hadn't moved and Jenny bit her lip. The
sounds came again, and this time Cherry yelled her
name. Jenny slipped inside.

After being outside, even in the fading light, it
felt black in the room. She shut the door trying to
help her eyes adjust. Small streams of light
illuminated a glow around the booth frames. Jenny
tiptoed closer to the stairs, avoiding the wreckage of
where she'd left Hugo.

Laughter sounded and Jenny looked at the broken booth. The shapes showed a pile of poles and the large chandelier dangling overhead, but no Hugo.

"Hugo?" Jenny called.

He laughed again, but her nerves were on such high alert that she couldn't place the location. It sounded like he was all around her.

Cherry's voice had gone quiet but she moved toward the stairs anyway.

"I wouldn't go up there. Maggie's making a new friend." Hugo's voice came from just past the stairwell and Jenny backed up.

"Hugo?" Maybe she could get him talking again. "You don't have to do this. No one died this time. Sally's going to be okay. Why don't you talk to her about what you really want? She probably didn't even know."

"Oh, she knew." Hugo's voice had gotten louder, but no one was there. Jenny backed up into the booth and circled around the poles. She needed a safe space, but she knew how easily every one of these booths could come down. Nowhere felt safe.

"Are you sure? The Sally I know wouldn't treat people like that." Jenny waited for his response before moving again.

When he spoke, his words came from the other side of the room. "Then you haven't been paying attention to her lies. She lied about Owen, she lied about her sister, she lied about Mickey's line, she even lied about you. And that's why you aren't getting out of here alive." Hugo appeared in front the booth.

Jenny took a quick step back, stumbling against one of the few metal poles still standing.

Hugo stalked closer, advancing slowly around the tumble of metal and fabric. Jenny shifted away, and Hugo came through the center of the booth instead. Jenny whimpered as he passed under the the chandelier hanging over the space where the settee had been. Jenny twisted the cross beam that was holding it in place. The hook jumped the track, and Hugo shielded himself as the large chandelier came down.

"Jenny!" Cherry's voice calling through the wreckage had never sounded so welcome.

"Cherry!" Jenny called back. "I'm still here!"

Light spilled through the building as Cherry led the police officers to where Jenny stood watching Hugo. He was pinned under the metal, and as the officers pulled the large fixture off of him, he turned to Jenny.

"Watch yourself. You can't get by on your lies forever."

Jenny flinched, and someone pulled him back.

"Did someone find Sally?" She was exhausted, and Cherry nodded.

Jenny let out a breath and leaned against Cherry's shoulder. "I can't wait for Ron to ask what I did today."

Hillary Doan Sperry

The white beard bounced against Ron's red suit, and he brushed a curl from Jenny's face. "Are you sure you want to do this, Mrs. Claus?"

"Of course I am."

The parade hadn't started yet, but the street was already lined with families and children. The little ones gathered up handfuls of the thin dusting of snow that had fallen overnight before the sunshine turned it to puddles.

Dressed in her red and white Mrs. Claus outfit, Jenny smiled and waved to people as she let Ron escort her to the rental property behind the Sewing Center, where Owen had told Jenny he'd be waiting. As they crossed the driveway, Owen jumped up from the steps.

"Jenny."

Jenny grinned and tightened her grip on the muff she held at her waist. "Mrs. Claus, thank you."

"My apologies, Mrs. Claus." Owen looked her over and Sally stood beside him. "Thanks for meeting us. It's been quite a week and, well, I wanted to apologize. If it weren't for you, Sally wouldn't be here and I could have lost exactly what I was trying so hard to save."

Sally stepped away from Owen. She smiled, though she was a little hesitant. "I can't thank you enough. I know we both lost people who were dear to us, and I was terrible in the process. All I can say is, I was

234

so confused and upset. I didn't know how to fix ar of it. And I couldn't." She looked up, her eyes brigh and hopeful. "Jenny, you changed everything for us. I don't know if you're still interested after everything you've been through, but we'd love to offer you a job as a designer for our team."

Jenny laughed. "You know I can't design, right? I'd be happy to take one of those pins though."

Sally held her hand out and produced a Harper Wovens Designer pin.

"Are you serious? I wasn't joking. I mean, I'd love to, but I don't think it would work out well." Jenny watched the pin glint in the sunlight and looked curiously at Sally.

Sally pinned the little token on Jenny's robe. "You would be fine. There are dozens of kinds of artists that create fabric. You just have to find the artwork you want to share. But either way, this is yours. You've earned a place on our team whenever you want it."

Jenny looked up at Ron, and he raised his eyebrows. The idea of being a designer had been in her head for so long that realizing she could actually do it unfurled a freedom and giddiness inside her. She laughed and turned back to Sally. "You know, I'm really happy where I am. But thank you. I'll treasure this."

Sally furrowed her brow. "I understand."

Jenny wasn't sure she did, but she straightened her bonnet and thought for a moment. "You should talk to Helen. I know she didn't want to do it this week, at now that things have settled down, she might be willing to reconsider it."

Owen grinned. "We already have. She signed a contract to start with a summer and winter line next year."

"Oh, that's great. I hope it works out for both of you."

Sally and Owen followed Jenny and Ron back to the parade route. From there, they parted ways and Mr. and Mrs. Claus made their way back to the parade head, where Ron helped Jenny into the vintage black Model T roadster that they would ride.

"I'm always amazed at what you can do with your fabric. How did you finish that so quickly?"

Jenny straightened the red and white quilt on her lap and leaned over, giving him a kiss.

"A little Christmas magic and a lot of good friends," Jenny said, thinking of all the running around and help it had taken to quilt and bind the redwork lemoyne star quilt that morning.

She'd get her filming in that afternoon and everything would work out beautifully. "Getting this finished so quickly makes me feel like a little bit of a superhero. It was pretty miraculous the way it all came together."

"I'm sure there are other people this week that would agree with that title. Though Mrs. Claus isn't your typical superhero." Ron moved to the front of the car and cranked the engine to get it going, then climbed in next to Jenny.

"What are you talking about? I can't imagine a

better superhero than Mrs. Claus. Who doesn't want to be saved by a girl who brings you presents and cookies when she's done helping? I think I'd feel better if the next time someone saved me, they also brought cookies."

Jenny straightened her cloak, the new Harper Wovens pin shining like a gold medal, and leaned against Ron's shoulder.

Jenny nodded. "That does sound nice."

He pulled the car into line with the other parade floats and children and leaned over to Jenny. "Just so you know, you can save me any day. I'll bring the cookies."

Acknowledgments

I have found the more I write the more I recognize the value of the amazing team that supports and creates with me. I need to mention them here (side note – this section is probably riddled with grammatical errors because I'm not having my editors read it first. This is all me baby.)

To my editors – Chasity Bradford, Tamara Fleming, Iris van de Pavert, Allyson Spony. You have all seen me at my worst and had the courage to speak up and help me see how I can be better.

Germancreative designed the beautiful cover A Body in Roadwork finally received with artwork by Ujala Shahid I cannot thank you ladies enough. I can't tell you how often I worried and searched to find someone who would help this book get the cover it deserved. I also want to acknowledge the talented artists who created beautiful covers that you may never see. It was quite a process finding the right one.

Thank you to my handsome, amazing, adoring, and supportive husband Q. Alex Sperry (hope you liked that hun!) and my family Allyson, Olivia, Alayna, Phoebe, and Jackson for the precious time and service you gave to support me as I wrote and struggled to focus. I have seen it and I love you for and apart from it. Thank you to my mother. It didn't matter how terrible the drafts have been that I sent you, you always see the beauty. I didn't know how desperately I needed that until I doubted and your encouraging words made all the difference.

I am all teary as I write this and it may have to do with the sleepless nights but I am so grateful for every one of you. If I missed someone I am so sorry and I blame it also on the sleepless nights. The support I've received is nothing less than miraculous. You amazing people have blessed my life. While thank you is not enough, it is all I have. So, Thank you. Thank you to my team and thank you to you, my readers. I hope you have the chance to fall in love with many more books about Hamilton and Jenny as we go forward. Maybe with a few less tears and sleepless nights. Happy quilting and happy reading.

—— Hillary

My name is Hillary Dawn Sperry. I'm a quilter and a writer among many other things that make up me. I love ice cream and chocolate cake and the glorious smell of walking through a fabric store!

My favorite color combo is turquoise and a soft coral. And I absolutely adore dreaming up strange new things for Cherry to wear when she's hanging out with Jenny in the Missouri Star Mystery books!

If you want to read more of my books check out your favorite library or online through my website hillarysperry.com; on the MSQC website or your favorite online retailer! Thanks for reading with me!

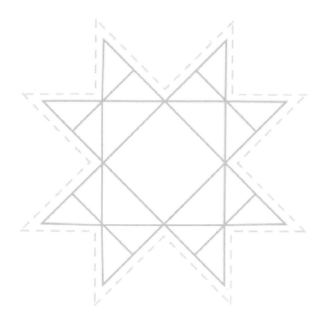

www.hillarysperry.com